Larry and Audr

Anointed to Heal

A Study Guide for Healing and Wholeness
from a Christian Perspective

Providence House Publishers
WWW.PROVIDENCEHOUSE.COM
FRANKLIN, TENNESSEE

Copyright 1997, 2007 by Lawrence L. Eddings and Audrey E. Eddings

All rights reserved. Written permission must be secured from the publisher to use or reproduce any part of this book, except for brief quotations in critical reviews or articles.

Printed in the United States of America

11   10   09   08   07   1   2   3   4   5

Library of Congress Control Number: 2007938817

ISBN: 978-1-57736-402-3

Cover and page design by LeAnna Massingille

Unless otherwise indicated, Scriptures are taken from HOLY BIBLE, NEW INTERNATIONAL VERSION®. Copyright © 1973, 1978, 1984 by International Bible Society. Used by permission of Zondervan Publishing House.

Scripture quotations marked NKJV are taken from the New King James Version®. Copyright © 1982 by Thomas Nelson, Inc. Used by permission. All rights reserved.

Scripture quotations marked KJV are taken from the Holy Bible, King James Version, Cambridge, 1796.

Scripture quotations marked NCV are taken from the Holy Bible, The New Century Version®. Copyright © 2005 by Thomas Nelson, Inc. Used by permission. All rights reserved.

Scripture quotations marked RSV are taken from the Revised Standard Version of the Bible, copyright 1952 [2nd edition, 1971] by the Division of Christian Education of the National Council of the Churches of Christ in the United States of America. Used by permission. All rights reserved.

PROVIDENCE HOUSE PUBLISHERS
238 Seaboard Lane • Franklin, Tennessee 37067
www.providencehouse.com
800-321-5692

The Spirit of the Lord is on me, because he has anointed me to preach good news to the poor. He has sent me to proclaim freedom for the prisoners, and recovery of sight for the blind, to release the oppressed, to proclaim the year of the Lord's favor.

—Luke 4:18–19

CONTENTS

PREFACE and ACKNOWLEDGMENTS ix

Introduction 1
  I. God is Our Comforter 3
  II. Sources of Affliction 9
  III. God Comforts Us in Our Affliction 17
  IV. The Holy Spirit: God's Promised Gift 21
  V. Baptism and the Holy Spirit 29
  VI. The Word of Knowledge 35
  VII. Healing the Human Spirit 47
VIII. Forgiveness and the Healing Process 55
  IX. Practicing Forgiveness 63
  X. Healing of Emotional Hurts 69
  XI. The Gift of Discernment 77
  XII. The Ministry of Deliverance 81
XIII. Physical Healing 91
XIV. The Physical Healing Process 97

APPENDIX: Facilitator's Guide for *Anointed to Heal* 105
BIBLIOGRAPHY 115
ABOUT THE AUTHORS 118

PREFACE

This book is written for the purpose of equipping persons to be in ministry to others who may have spiritual, emotional, physical, and/or relational needs.

It is designed to be used in adult Sunday school classes, small study groups, home fellowships, and/or other Christian growth groups within the local church. The material is especially helpful for those churches with a desire to incorporate a healing ministry as one of the vital ministries of their church.

The material is offered in a format that allows for discussion during the presentation of material in the chapter or at the conclusion of the session. If the book is used as a study resource, it is suggested that approximately twenty minutes of each period be allotted for discussion and/or workshop. Facilitators are encouraged to use stories with which they are familiar to illustrate the material being taught.

ACKNOWLEDGMENTS

Any endeavor to prepare materials for the publishing of a book should involve the work of persons in addition to the authors. Therefore, we would like to express deep appreciation and acknowledgment for those who have contributed to this work. We acknowledge the gracious help of those who are also involved in healing ministry and from whom we have gained insights, practicum, and ongoing encouragement. Many of these are listed in the bibliography.

This book was born out of ministry with the people of First United Methodist Church in Tulsa, Oklahoma. Dr. James Buskirk, senior pastor at the time, and the church graciously helped in providing the means for which this material could be used as curriculum in adult Sunday school classes for studying healing and wholeness.

We would like to recognize researcher and resource person, Miss Anne Key, who provided many excellent ideas and personal insights. We would also like to extend gratitude to Sally Havens, a longtime friend and colleague in ministry, who gave great assistance in editing the manuscript and helping to clarify topics for easier reading.

We express appreciation to those on the teaching staff of Wind of the Spirit Ministries who have helped make practical application of the material a reality in Healing Academies. These include Revs. Taylor and Jenny Gallman, Rev. Davis Hylkema, and Anne Key.

We acknowledge the valuable help of our staff persons Dick and Mary Weigel, Georgia Mattson, and others, who are ever-present sources of encouragement, counsel, and reminders of deadlines. To all, we express our gratitude and heartfelt thanks.

We give special thanks to Nancy Wise and the editorial staff of Providence House Publishers for their careful and thorough work in helping prepare the book for publication.

Above all, we give thanks to God and our Lord Jesus Christ for granting us the privilege of working under the direction of God's Holy Spirit in the ministry of healing and wholeness. We pray that this book will bless many and bring honor to the name of our Lord.

INTRODUCTION

Anointed to Heal finds its source in Jesus—His life and ministry. At the very beginning of His ministry, He stood in the synagogue in Nazareth to read from the scroll of the prophet Isaiah:

The Spirit of the Lord is on me, because he has anointed me to preach good news to the poor. He has sent me to proclaim freedom for the prisoners, and recovery of sight for the blind, to release the oppressed, to proclaim the year of the Lord's favor.
—**Luke 4:18–19 (Isaiah 61:1–2)**

To be anointed is to be set apart for sacred purposes. When prophets, priests, and kings were anointed in the years before Christ, they were set apart, authorized, and empowered to do that work which God had assigned them to do.

The prophets were anointed to proclaim or speak forth God's Word. The priests were anointed to perform the ministries related to the temple and to lead the community of faith in matters of their relationship with God. The kings were anointed to rule the people of God with justice. All were anointed and set apart to act as God's spokespersons and emissaries.

In the kingdom of God, one who has not been given a particular responsibility has no authority to do it, and thus is not anointed to do it. However, when responsibility is given, authority is also given, through the anointing, to carry it out. Thus, the prophets, priests, and kings were authorized and empowered to carry out the work of the community that had been assigned to them by God.

Jesus came as Prophet, Priest, King, Son of God, Son of Man, Redeemer, Savior, Deliverer, Healer, and Lord.

Jesus was anointed by the Holy Spirit of God.

- He was set apart for the sacred purpose of preaching good news of the kingdom of God to the poor. He had the authority and the power to do it.

- He was also anointed—authorized and empowered—to proclaim freedom for captives, recovery of sight to the blind, and release for the oppressed.

- He had the authority and power to heal. He preached the gospel and healed the sick.

- He had the power and authority, through His anointing, to support what He said with what He did.

Jesus preached the kingdom of God, healed the sick, forgave sins, and delivered people from demonic oppression (Luke 4:18–19). In turn, He gave that same authority to His disciples who walked alongside Him. He sent them out to preach the good news of the kingdom and to heal the sick (Luke 9:1–2).

Through the Scriptures, the church (the body of Christ) has been anointed—set apart, authorized, and empowered—by the Holy Spirit to also preach the gospel, heal the sick, forgive sins, and deliver people from demonic oppression (Luke 10:1–20; Matt. 28:1–20).

The contemporary church is in a position to take up once again the sacred task that has been assigned by God and anointed by the Holy Spirit.

Anointed to Heal is designed to equip persons to fulfill that ministry for which they have been or can be anointed by the Spirit. May this be the time when once again, we, like Jesus, "proclaim the year of the Lord's favor" (Luke 4:19).

1. GOD IS OUR COMFORTER

This chapter affirms that God is our Comforter, not our afflicter. God is our Creator, not our destroyer. Jesus is our Advocate, not our adversary. The Holy Spirit, in particular, is our Comforter, not our accuser. God is the God of compassion who enters into our pain and suffering in the person of Jesus Christ and empowers us to overcome through the indwelling Holy Spirit.

God comforts people in their afflictions so that they may comfort others in their afflictions. God's healing power is demonstrated in the life of Jesus. About 90–95 percent of Jesus' ministry involved healing of some kind.

In order to understand the God of compassion, the God to whom we pray and with whom we commune, it is important to understand and discover the nature of God as revealed to us in Scripture and through the life of Jesus.

SCRIPTURE:

Comfort, comfort my people, says your God. Speak tenderly to Jerusalem, and proclaim to her that her hard service has been completed, that her sin has been paid for, that she has received from the Lord's hand double for all her sins.

—Isaiah 40:1–2

Praise be to the God and Father of our Lord Jesus Christ, the Father of compassion and the God of all comfort, who comforts us in all our troubles, so that we can comfort those in any trouble with the comfort we ourselves have received from God. For just as the sufferings of Christ flow over into our lives, so also through Christ our comfort overflows.

—2 Corinthians 1:3–5

You know what has happened throughout Judea, beginning in Galilee after the baptism that John preached—how God anointed Jesus of Nazareth with the Holy Spirit and power, and how he went around doing good and healing all who were under the power of the devil, because God was with him. We are witnesses of everything he did in the country of the Jews and in Jerusalem.

—Acts 10:37–39

Additional Scripture Readings: Isaiah 40:11; Isaiah 49:13–16; Matthew 6:7–15; Luke 11:1–8; Hebrews 2:14–18

As persons involved in ministry, especially in the healing ministry, we dare to believe that God is for us, not against us, and "if God is for us, who can be against us?" (Rom. 8:31).

Having said that God is for us, we acknowledge that we live in a world where sin, sickness, disease, suffering, and death are realities with which we are confronted each day. There isn't a person who has not been touched in some way by one of these realities.

Consequently, as humans, we ask the question, "Why?" Then we seek to identify a possible source of the predicament by asking, "God, why?"

Then, many people often endeavor to spiritualize the experience by saying something like, "God is doing this to me—or allowing this to happen to me—in order that I may be stronger, or to teach me a lesson, or to develop my faith or character."

Consequently, there develops the subtle, yet strong tendency to believe that God afflicts us, and in doing so, God has a noble purpose. That purpose is to comfort us and strengthen us by the experience of affliction.

These incorrect assumptions about God's character can be refuted by scriptural affirmations that reveal the true nature of God and which are in harmony with the revelation of the nature of God as seen in the life of Jesus. These affirmations and revelations are crucial to a positive and effective healing ministry.

The first affirmation is, "God is not our afflicter! God is our Comforter!" "Praise be to the God and Father of our Lord Jesus Christ, the Father of compassion and the God of all comfort" (2 Cor. 1:3).

God is the source of compassion—its Creator, the One who brought compassion into being, the Father of compassion.

Compassion means "to suffer with." Com(with) passion(suffer). Compassion is the ability to enter into another's suffering and affliction and to feel what is being felt by that person.

Such godly compassion is perfectly illustrated in the life of Jesus Christ, for in Him, God entered into our human predicament, suffering, and life experiences.

> Since the children have flesh and blood, he too shared in their humanity . . . he had to be made like his brothers in every way, in order that he might become a merciful and faithful high priest in service to God, and that he might make atonement for the sins of the people. Because he himself suffered when he was tempted, he is able to help those who are being tempted.
> —Hebrews 2:14, 17–18

Jesus understands the need for compassion in the midst of people's suffering.

Matthew 15:32 expresses this when Jesus saw the hungry crowds and said, "I have compassion for these people." He knew their hunger for He shared in it. He fed them. Jesus was filled with compassion for the leper; He healed him (Mark 1:41).

To those who were hurting and needed healing as well as to persons who were hungry and needed feeding, Jesus truly demonstrated that God is a God of compassion. At no time did Jesus tell people to stay sick and learn lessons that God had for them. He felt their afflictions and He met their needs.

God is the Father of compassion and the God of all comfort. It is no accident that the Holy Spirit is called the Paraclete, the Comforter, the one who comes alongside and helps, or "comes with strength." Com(with) forte(strength) (John 14). That is God's nature; God's presence is the source of all comfort. "I am the Lord, who heals you" (Exod. 15:26).

Comfort is the **outflow** of compassion; it means "with strength," "to walk along beside and help." Compassion enters into the affliction; comfort provides us strength and fortifies us to walk through it.

It is true that God's ways are not our ways.

> *"For my thoughts are not your thoughts, neither are your ways my ways," declares the Lord. "As the heavens are higher than the earth, so are my ways higher than your ways and my thoughts than your thoughts."*
>
> —Isaiah 55:8–9

God's ways and thoughts are **higher** than ours, not lower. If I, who am evil, know how to do good to my children, how much more does God know how to do good to His children? (Luke 11:13).

God can teach us in adversity and affliction. Our faith is tried in the fires of tribulation. Such testing of our faith does develop perseverance and character (James 1:3; Rom. 5:3–5).

That is the good that God brings out of difficult situations, for "in all things God works for the good of those who love him, who have been called according to his purpose" (Rom. 8:28). However, God is not the adversary. God is the advocate as demonstrated in the life of Jesus. "We have an Advocate with the Father, Jesus Christ the righteous" (1 John 2:1 NKJV).

Since God is the Comforter and not the afflicter, who or what, then, is the source of our affliction? We'll discuss that in the next chapter, and once we understand the source of our affliction, we can minister more effectively in and to the situation at hand.

The God to Whom We Pray

> *I am the Lord who brought you up out of Egypt to be your God; therefore be holy, because I am holy.* [handwritten: ♪ Take Time to Be Holy]
>
> —Leviticus 11:45

> *When you pray, go into your room, close the door and pray to your Father, who is unseen. Then your Father, who sees what is done in secret, will reward you.*
>
> —Matthew 6:6

> *So I say to you: Ask and it will be given to you; seek and you will find; knock and the door will be opened to you. For everyone who asks receives; he who seeks finds; and to him who knocks, the door will be opened. Which of you fathers, if your son asks for a fish, will give him a snake instead? Or if he asks for an egg, will give him a scorpion? If you then, though you are evil, know how to give good gifts to your children, how much more will your Father in heaven give the Holy Spirit to those who ask him!*
>
> —Luke 11:9–13

If we are to have an effective and productive prayer life and ministry, then it is important to gain yet an even deeper understanding of the God in whom we believe and the God to whom we pray. Scripture reinforces the idea of God's nature as Comforter and not afflicter. If we are to have hope in God—hope being absolute confidence and trust—then we must know something of the One in whom we have that absolute confidence and trust.

Holy

First, Scripture informs us that God is holy. Throughout the Old Testament, it is either stated outright or implied that God is a holy God. Leviticus 11:44 states, "I am the Lord your God; consecrate yourselves and be holy, because I am holy."

The word holy means to be separate and set apart for sacred purposes. It carries with it the idea of being different. God is set apart and different from all else. God is the great "I Am." There are no other gods. There were none before God nor will there be any after God, for God is the Alpha and the Omega—the beginning and the end (Isa. 46:8–10).

God is holy. God is omniscient, all-knowing and righteous. God is absolute purity and perfection. God knows our needs even before we ask (Matt. 6:8).

Knowing this, we can confidently communicate with the One who is able to do immeasurably more than anything we could ask or imagine; He who is not overwhelmed by the size of our requests, nor influenced by the magnitude of our praise. We pray to the One for whom nothing is impossible and whose will for us is far greater than anything we could will for ourselves. We never have to ask, "God, do you not know the need?" God knows!

Spirit

Scripture also tells us that God is Spirit (John 4:24). Therefore, God's nature is not only holy but also spirit. Spirit is given form in the person of Jesus. God's Holy Spirit is the Spirit of the Holy God who is perfectly revealed in Jesus, who is God incarnate in the flesh. Incarnate means to be given form—that which is invisible is made visible; that which is without form is given form; that which is spirit is given flesh.

Jesus told the disciples that it was for their good that He must go away, for then He would send the Holy Spirit to be with them (John 16:5–7). When Jesus was on earth in the flesh, He was limited by place, time, and circumstances. He could be in only one place at one time dealing with one circumstance. However, since God sent His Holy Spirit, the Spirit is now present at all times in all places and in all circumstances at the same time.

Consequently, we have a God who is not limited in any way. God is as near as the air we breathe, for we are indwelt by God's Spirit. And too, we may intercede for loved ones in another place and God is there with them even as we pray. God is not "out there" or "over there" or "somewhere," but God is the great "I Am Present."

While God is present at all times in all places and in all circumstances, there are occasions when God's manifest presence becomes real. That is, God "shows up" and God's presence is very evident. God's presence is experienced in very real ways here on earth. Perhaps one of the best examples is the resurrected Jesus' appearance on the road to Damascus where Saul encountered him (Acts 9:3–5). The omnipresent God manifested His presence in that encounter.

God's manifest presence also becomes real when persons are healed, experience forgiveness, or discover deliverance from a sin that has plagued them for much of their lives. In prayer, we never have to ask, "God, where are you?" God is here!

Consuming Fire

In addition, Scripture clearly reminds us that God is a consuming fire (Heb. 12:28–29). Throughout Scripture, fire is used to symbolize purification and cleansing. Fire burns away dross and purifies the element, whether silver or gold. Fire also burns away and purifies that which is dross in human life. John the Baptist proclaimed that after him there would come one who would "baptize you with the Holy Spirit and fire" (Luke 3:16).

Fire may also be symbolic of power and authority. God has the power and authority to purify and cleanse. God has the power to forgive and heal. God has the authority to judge and deliver.

Thus, our communion is with One who has all authority, all power, all ability to do that which is to be done according to God's perfect will. God is able to make good on the promises which have been made in the Scriptures, all of which find their "yes" in Jesus (2 Cor. 1:20).

Therefore, when we are in prayer or in ministry with another, we never have to ask, "God, are you able to do this?" God is able! (Eph. 3:20–21).

Light

In 1 John 1:5, we are reminded that "God is light; in him there is no darkness at all." Light in this setting means enlightenment. In John's gospel, we read, "The true light that gives light to every man was coming into the world" (1:9). And again, "Light has come into the world, but men loved darkness instead of light because their deeds were evil" (3:19).

God is the God who does not hide, but is continually being revealed through Jesus, the incarnate Word; through the Holy Spirit, the living Word; through the Scriptures, the written Word. Consequently, no one has to search for God but need only to acknowledge God's presence and receive that which God has for him or her. When God reveals truth relative to circumstances or events, then one may pray with confidence and assurance, with the mind and also with the spirit.

In prayer, we never have to ask of God, "Don't you understand what I'm going through?" God does and will help us see how He is working in the circumstances for our good.

Love

God is love. Perhaps the greatest attribute of God's nature that impacts us as human beings is that of love. First John 4:7–21 affirms this nature of God. God's love is an unconditional, sacrificial, and eternal love. It is not influenced or changed by circumstances, events, disobedience, sin, or anything else that would seek to destroy the relationship that God desires to have with people.

Love must have an object, and people are the object of God's love. That love moves the heart of God to comfort, console, bless, give grace, forgive, heal, and welcome into right relationship. Therefore, we never have to ask of God the question, "God, don't you care?" God does care because God loves. The one praying, as well as the one for whom prayer is said, is the object of God's love.

By understanding, as best we can, the nature of God as portrayed in Scripture, we are helped to know that God truly is the "Father of compassion and the God of all comfort" (2 Cor. 1:3). God is our Comforter, not our afflicter; God is our Advocate, not our adversary; God is for us, not against us. And, if God is for us, who can be against us? (Rom. 8:31).

IDEAS FOR REFLECTION

Please share at a level that is comfortable for you.

What is demonstrated in the life of Jesus that would help us understand that God is a compassionate and comforting God? That is, how did Jesus demonstrate God's compassion and comfort?

Discuss the attributes of the nature of God as recorded in Scripture:

- Holy
- Spirit
- Consuming Fire
- Light
- Love

How are these attributes manifested in the life of Jesus?
What is there about the nature of God that is reassuring to us as we pray?

II. SOURCES OF AFFLICTION

If God is, in fact, not the source of affliction (as we affirmed in the first chapter), then who or what is? Let's explore the various sources of affliction revealed in Scripture. We will also discuss the affliction and suffering that we experience as a result of living in this world.

There are several kinds of suffering.

- The first type of suffering comes from disobedience to God's laws. That disobedience finds its source in three places: Satan, others, and self.

- The second kind of suffering is that which comes because of obedience to God's laws. Obedience to God's laws brings us into conflict with the laws of this world—kingdom principles in conflict with world principles—thus, suffering for righteousness' sake.

- The third kind of suffering comes through life's circumstances.

God works to bring forgiveness and deliverance in the first kind of suffering, to bring blessing and strength in the second, and to bring healing in the third.

SCRIPTURE:

To the woman he said, "I will greatly increase your pains in childbearing; with pain you will give birth to children. Your desire will be for your husband, and he will rule over you." To Adam he said, "Because you listened to your wife and ate from the tree about which I commanded you, 'You must not eat of it,' Cursed is the ground because of you; through painful toil you will eat of it all the days of your life. It will produce thorns and thistles for you, and you will eat the plants of the field. By the sweat of your brow you will eat your food until you return to the ground, since from it you were taken; for dust you are and to dust you will return."

—**Genesis 3:16–19**

If the world hates you, keep in mind that it hated me first. If you belonged to the world, it would love you as its own. As it is, you do not belong to the world, but I have chosen you out of the world. That is why the world hates you. Remember the words I spoke to you: "No servant is greater than his master." If they persecuted me, they will persecute you also. If they obeyed my teaching, they will obey yours also. They will treat you this way because of my name, for they do not know the One who sent me. If I had not come and spoken to them, they would not be guilty of sin. Now, however, they have no excuse for their sin. He who hates me hates my Father as well. If I had not done among them what no one else did, they would not be guilty of sin. But now they have seen these miracles, and yet they have hated both me and my Father. But this is to fulfill what is written in their Law: "They hated me without reason."

—John 15:18–25

Dear friends, do not be surprised at the painful trial you are suffering, as though something strange were happening to you. But rejoice that you participate in the sufferings of Christ, so that you may be overjoyed when his glory is revealed. If you are insulted because of the name of Christ, you are blessed, for the Spirit of glory and of God rests on you. If you suffer, it should not be as a murderer or thief or any other kind of criminal, or even as a meddler. However, if you suffer as a Christian, do not be ashamed, but praise God that you bear that name. For it is time for judgment to begin with the family of God; and if it begins with us, what will the outcome be for those who do not obey the gospel of God? And, "If it is hard for the righteous to be saved, what will become of the ungodly and the sinner?" So then, those who suffer according to God's will should commit themselves to their faithful Creator and continue to do good.

—1 Peter 4:12–19

Additional Scripture Readings: Isaiah 53; Jonah 1; Acts 5:1–11; Romans 5:1–5

First, a word must be said about pain that is felt in our bodies. Physical pain is a God-given gift to provide for health and wholeness in our bodies. Pain serves as an early warning system to let us know when something is wrong in our bodies—when we have been wounded and when areas of our anatomy that are not visible to us need attention.

Pain serves to move us to pay attention; it is one overt way our body has of informing us that all is not well. Persons who do not experience pain are in grave danger, for then their bodies have no way of signaling danger.

We need to have a prayer of praise and thanksgiving on our lips to God for the gift of pain. Suffering, on the other hand, is

- an affliction
- a consequence of trauma
- out-of-control pain
- multifaceted
- a result of our own pain or the pain of another.

It must also be said that suffering or affliction has with it the dimension of mystery and to not recognize the mystery would be presumptuous. "We know in part because we can see only in part for we look into a glass darkly" (1 Cor. 13:12, paraphrased).

For example, who can describe the hurt or have answers for the young couple whose six-month-old baby daughter dies of Sudden Infant Death Syndrome (SIDS)? Or the couple who, after thirty-five years of apparently happy marriage, choose to get a divorce? Or for the family of the fourteen-year-old girl who becomes pregnant? Who has the wisdom and insight to explain the intangible elements involved in these? Yet these experiences occur to people of faith and to people without faith.

In suffering and affliction, we must acknowledge the mystery and simply say that we do not understand all things. Nevertheless, we do understand some things and have some knowledge regarding much of life's tribulations and hurt. We must use the knowledge we have, under the direction of the Holy Spirit, to be instruments of healing for God's people in God's world.

Suffering and Affliction Caused by Disobedience

While much mystery surrounds suffering, we do know that one source of our suffering is disobedience.

God has established certain laws for our good; they are designed to bring wholeness into our lives. These laws are not meant to restrict us, but to bring fulfillment. To disobey these laws results in suffering and affliction.

God has established **spiritual laws** to bring us into and keep us in right relationship with God and with those around us.

God has established laws that we:

- "Love the Lord your God with all your heart and with all your soul and with all your strength" (Deut. 6:5).

- "Love your neighbor as yourself" (Matt. 22:37–39).

- "[Forgive] each other, just as in Christ God forgave you" (Eph. 4:32).

These are spiritual laws designed to bring spiritual wholeness and health to our spirits and to our relationships. To keep them is to enjoy wholeness and freedom; disobeying them impacts our relationship with God and others.

To disobey God's spiritual laws results in an unloving, uncaring, and hateful attitude toward God and others. Suffering is another consequence of that disobedience. For example, to disobey the law of forgiveness results in unforgiveness, bitterness, resentment, broken relations, and often physical illness.

God has also established **family laws** that are designed for wholeness in the family circle.

- "Children, obey your parents in the Lord, for this is right. Honor your father and mother—which is the first commandment with a promise—that it may go well with you and that you may enjoy long life on the earth" (Eph. 6:1–3).

- "Fathers, do not exasperate your children; instead, bring them up in the training and instruction of the Lord" (Eph. 6:4).

- "[Husbands and wives,] submit to one another out of reverence for Christ" (Eph. 5:21).

When these laws are obeyed, things go fairly well in the family circle. When these basic family laws are disobeyed, the result is child abuse, spousal abuse, parental abuse, incest, the breakdown of the family unit, and the devaluing of the worth of persons with whom we are most closely related.

God has established **societal laws** that are designed to help us live together in the human family in safety and with concern for each other: "You shall not kill; you shall not commit adultery; you shall not lie; you shall not steal; you shall not covet your neighbor's house" (Exod. 20:13–16, paraphrased).

These laws are all designed to help us have an appropriate attitude toward those who share planet Earth with us. Disobedience of these and other societal laws results in injury, suffering, and, in many cases, death.

Ignoring traffic lights, driving while drinking, killing, stealing, drug trafficking, injustice, and prejudice all affect the health of a society, and, as a result, people suffer.

God has established **moral laws** to guide us in our interpersonal relations: "You shall not commit adultery" (Exod. 20:14), and "Put to death . . . sexual immorality, impurity, lust, evil desires, and greed . . . anger, rage, malice, slander, and filthy language . . ." (Col. 3:5, 8).

These laws are all designed to help us honor one another as persons of worth. The disobedience of these moral laws not only has a negative effect upon our own bodies, but also upon appropriate value systems that work to provide healthy relationships in a societal structure.

The Center for Disease Control (CDC, Atlanta) reports that there are presently twenty-six sexually transmitted diseases (STDs) for which there is no known cure. They cause pain and suffering. They can be prevented by choosing to live in a monogamous relationship.

God has also established **health laws** that enable us to live relatively healthy lives by paying attention to how we eat and how we treat our bodies.

Our bodies are temples of the Holy Spirit. What we eat, how we exercise, how we think, how we rest, and the pace of our work all correspond with obeying or disobeying God's laws designed to give us healthy bodies.

Disobedience to these basic laws results in sickness, pain, and sometimes, death. To ignore the reality of diseases and the proper precautions against them is to court disaster in our bodies. To ignore good eating and exercise habits also invites disaster and suffering.

One source of suffering, then, is the disobedience of God's basic laws which are designed for our spiritual, emotional, relational, and physical health.

Root Causes of Disobedience That Bring Suffering

Disobedience finds its root in one of three sources:

- Satan
- Others
- Self

The first source is Satan, who, in Scripture, is variously called the adversary, the devil, the slanderer, and the deceiver.

Jesus referred to the devil as a liar and the father of lies; lying is his native tongue (John 8:44). A person who bears false witness or does not deal with the truth, then, would be under the influence of Satan.

Jesus also spoke of the devil as being a murderer and the one who comes to "steal and kill and destroy" (John 8:44, 10:10).

The apostle Peter describes the adversary as one who "prowls around like a roaring lion looking for someone to devour" (1 Pet. 5:8). He cautions his readers to "resist him, standing firm in the faith, because you know that your brothers throughout the world are undergoing the same kind of sufferings" (1 Pet. 5:9).

The apostle Paul sees Satan as the deceiver for he is able to disguise himself as an angel of light (2 Cor. 11:14). Through lies, deceit, and temptation, Satan endeavors to lead persons into disobedience that results in spiritual, emotional, physical, and relational suffering.

Therefore, one source of disobedience that leads to suffering is the devil. To not acknowledge the presence and reality of such an adversary is to prepare ourselves for being ineffective and unproductive in the healing ministry or in maintaining our own spiritual, emotional, and physical well-being.

A second source for disobedience that leads to suffering is found in **others**. That is, another person's disobedience can lead to our own suffering. For example, in 1983 our family experienced the tragedy of losing our first-born, six-year-old grandson in a horseback riding accident while his family was on vacation. The owner of the little dude ranch disobeyed certain basic safety laws regarding animals which resulted in our grandson's death. The pony on which our grandson was riding had not been broken to riding, and yet the lives of children were put at risk for the purpose of making money. The man's disobedience has caused untold suffering to our family.

There are times when we suffer because of another's disobedience of certain basic laws which are essential to physical, emotional, and relational health and wholeness.

Drivers of automobiles who do not stop at stop signs or fail to yield right-of-ways; persons who are careless with guns or intentionally use weapons to injure others; people who misuse power in their positions of leadership; or those who sexually harass others or abuse children—these persons inflict pain and suffering on others because of their disobedience of God's basic moral laws.

We suffer because another person is disobedient and we become the victim of their disobedience.

A third source for disobedience that results in suffering is **self**. One cannot always identify the source of disobedience as Satan or someone else; sometimes, the source is self.

There are times when one disobeys certain laws that have been established by God for good and the consequence is hurt and affliction imposed on self. Wrong choices often result in negative consequences.

We disobey God's health laws and the result is a sick body. We disregard God's basic moral laws and the result is moral degradation.

The apostle Paul states: "Do not be deceived: God cannot be mocked. A man reaps what he sows. The one who sows to please his sinful nature, from that nature will reap destruction; the one who sows to please the Spirit, from the Spirit will reap eternal life" (Gal. 6:7–8).

And, too, we must always acknowledge the real possibility that our disobedience may cause another to suffer. We can no longer be deceived by the myth that our behavior has no negative effect upon others and our decisions harm no one but ourselves. We are social beings and our behavior has a great and profound effect upon others around us.

The tragic and epidemic spread of the disease of Acquired Immune Deficiency Syndrome (AIDS) indicates once again that what we do as individuals impacts our human family's health and wholeness—even on an international scale.

In addition, our decision to ignore God's call for compassion and assistance for those who suffer from the disease only results in adding to their pain and suffering.

Suffering and affliction, therefore, find their source in disobedience of God's basic laws regarding health and wholeness in our spiritual, emotional, physical, and relational being, and disobedience finds its source in Satan, in others, and in ourselves.

Affliction That Comes from Obedience to God's Laws

However, there is also suffering, affliction, and pain that come as the result of obeying those same laws that God has established for our good.

Suffering that comes from obedience to God's laws is clearly illustrated by stories of those who have endeavored to live by the standards of the kingdom of God in an environment hostile to those laws.

Jesus, John the Baptist, the early disciples, the early church, and believers down through the centuries all experienced this type of affliction and suffering.

When the kingdom standards conflict with the standards of the world, the result is often spiritual, emotional, physical, and relational suffering.

Jesus warned His disciples:

> *If the world hates you, keep in mind that it hated me first. If you belonged to the world, it would love you as its own. As it is, you do not belong to the world, but I have chosen you out of the world. That is why the world hates you. . . . If they persecuted me, they will persecute you also.*
> **—John 15:18–20**

He also warned them: "In this world you will have trouble. But take heart! I have overcome the world" (John 16:33).

Jesus suffered, not because of any disobedience, but because of His perfect obedience to God's will for His life and ministry. God's will was uppermost in His mind, and doing that will often brought Jesus into direct conflict with the standards of this world or with other religious standards. This is the "suffering for righteousness sake" about which Jesus spoke in the Sermon on the Mount:

> *Blessed are those who are persecuted [for righteousness' sake], for theirs is the kingdom of heaven. Blessed are you when people insult you, persecute you and falsely say all kinds of evil against you because of me. Rejoice and be glad, because great is your reward in heaven, for in the same way they persecuted the prophets who were before you.*
> **—Matthew 5:10–12**

For example, we know a woman who attended a weekend conference on the Holy Spirit. She remarked that when (not if, but when) her particular religious sect found out that she had attended the retreat, she would be disfellowshipped. This meant that she would experience total isolation from the religious community and from her family members. In endeavoring to know more of God and broaden her understanding of God's place in her life, she was destined to face persecution and loss of relationships that were dear to her. In a later meeting with her, she disclosed that she had indeed been disfellowshipped and lost all contact and relationship with her family and her religious group.

Not only the world's standards, but the standards of other religious bodies and Christian individuals can bring affliction and suffering into the life of that person who endeavors to be obedient to God's laws in his or her life.

According to David Barrett in the *World Christian Encyclopedia*, because of their obedience to their faith in God, approximately one thousand Christians are martyred per day throughout the world—persons suffering and dying because of their obedience to God's claim upon their lives through Jesus Christ.

Suffering Caused by Circumstances

Often persons suffer because of illness that comes upon them through no fault of their own or of anyone else. Suffering can also come from circumstances in which we find ourselves involved.

A leper came to Jesus and begged to be made clean. He suffered a physical malady caused by bacterium that attacks the nerve endings, resulting in the loss of the sense of pain. The disease was not the result of sin, disobedience, or wrong choices. Rather, it was caused by exposure to the bacteria.

The man who was brought to Jesus by his friends was paralyzed and could not walk. His paralysis may have been caused by an accident, the result of wrong choices, or perhaps even a sin in his life—as Jesus spoke forgiveness to him as part of his healing. We are not told the circumstances of his paralysis. However, we do know that this suffering came as a result of circumstances that he had faced, perhaps even circumstances related to his birth.

As Jesus and His disciples walked along, they saw a man who had been born blind. There is every indication that this blindness happened while his body was developing in his mother's womb. It was not the result of sin or wrong choices, obedience or disobedience. It was a circumstance of his birth.

A man with leprosy came to him and begged him on his knees, "If you are willing, you can make me clean." Filled with compassion, Jesus reached out his hand and touched the man. "I am willing," he said. "Be clean!" Immediately the leprosy left him and he was cured.
—Mark 1:40–42

A few days later, when Jesus again entered Capernaum, the people heard that he had come home. So many gathered that there was no room left, not even outside the door, and he preached the word to them. Some men came, bringing to him a paralytic, carried by four of them. Since they could not get him to Jesus because of the crowd, they made an opening in the roof above Jesus and, after digging through it, lowered the mat the paralyzed man was lying on. When Jesus saw their faith, he said to the paralytic, "Son, your sins are forgiven." . . . But that you may know that the Son of Man has authority on earth to forgive sins. . . ." He said to the paralytic, "I tell you, get up, take your mat and go home." He got up, took his mat and walked out in full view of them all. This amazed everyone and they praised God, saying, "We have never seen anything like this!"
—Mark 2:1–12

As he went along, he saw a man blind from birth. His disciples asked him, "Rabbi, who sinned, this man or his parents, that he was born blind?" "Neither this man nor his parents sinned," said Jesus, "but this happened so that the work of God might be displayed in his life."
—John 9:1–3

There are occasions in our own lives wherein we suffer because of circumstances in which we find ourselves.

We live in an imperfect world where viruses, germs, accidents, and incidents happen that bring hurt. None of these are premeditated, planned, caused, or inflicted; they happen because we live in a world where they exist and we come into contact with them.

Germs exist, bones break, diseases attack, and death stalks. There are precautions that can be taken to prevent them; nevertheless, the circumstances still arise that bring about physical and emotional sickness and hurt that are not a mystery, that are not caused by anyone's disobedience, and that are not the result of Satan's influence. They are circumstances of this earthly life.

Suffering can find its source in the disobedience of God's laws. It can also come as we endeavor to be obedient to those same laws and, as a result, come into conflict with the world around us. Finally, many of the circumstances related to this life can bring affliction.

IDEAS FOR REFLECTION

Please share at a level that is comfortable for you.

1. What is the value of pain?

2. What are some differences between pain and suffering?

3. How are God's laws designed for our good?

4. Discuss the sources of suffering: disobedience, obedience, and circumstances.

5. How do we suffer through disobedience?

6. How do we suffer through obedience?

7. What are some of the circumstances that cause us to suffer?

8. How have you experienced these in your own life?

III. GOD COMFORTS US IN OUR AFFLICTION

In the first two chapters we dealt with the truth that God is our Comforter and also with the fact that affliction and suffering come from a source other than God.

Now we will explore the various ways in which God ministers to us in the midst of our afflictions regardless of the source, bringing healing and wholeness into our lives. This exploration will underscore the fact that "in all things God works for the good of those who love him, who have been called according to his purpose" (Rom. 8:28).

We will also discover that God comforts us "so that we can comfort those in any trouble with the comfort we ourselves have received from God" (2 Cor. 1:4). This pattern is throughout Scripture. We are healed that we may be in ministry to others who need healing. God told Abraham that he was blessed to be a blessing (Gen. 12:2). In the same way, we are blessed to be a blessing.

SCRIPTURE:

Praise be to the God and Father of our Lord Jesus Christ, the Father of compassion and the God of all comfort, who comforts us in all our troubles, **so that** *we can comfort those in any trouble with the comfort we ourselves have received from God.*

—**2 Corinthians 1:3–4 (authors' emphasis)**

Jesus' Response to Our Suffering

One of the great truths of Scripture is that when we experience suffering and affliction in our lives, God comforts.

Scripture asserts that Jesus is the "radiance of God's glory and the exact representation of his being" (Heb. 1:3). Jesus brought comfort to the suffering.

Scripture also states that "the Son can do nothing by himself; he can do only what he sees his Father doing, because whatever the Father does the Son also does" (John 5:19).

Therefore, the response of Jesus to human suffering and affliction—at whatever level—is the response of God. Jesus' response is God's response. The two are the same.

Satanic Influence

When suffering came as the result of satanic influence, Jesus delivered people from the power and influence of the demonic. Approximately 25 percent of Jesus' ministry involved deliverance from bondage to Satan and demonic forces.

- Jesus delivered the demoniac at Gadara (Luke 8:26–39).
- Jesus healed the woman who had been crippled by a spirit for eighteen years (Luke 13:10–16).
- Jesus delivered the boy with the evil spirit (Luke 9:37–43).

Other People's Disobedience

When suffering was caused by other people's disobedience, Jesus had compassion and comforted the afflicted one.

- Jesus healed a man born blind. The healed man was ultimately thrown out of the temple by the religious rulers. Jesus found him and brought comfort to him (John 9).

Personal Disobedience

When persons suffered because of their own disobedience, Jesus forgave and brought reconciliation.

- A woman was caught in the act of adultery that brought suffering and the real possibility of death. Jesus did not condemn her but restored her sense of self-worth. "Woman, where are they? Has no one condemned you?" "No one, sir," she said. "Then neither do I condemn you," Jesus declared. "Go now and leave your life of sin" (John 8:10–11).
- Zacchaeus was a hated tax collector who caused others to suffer but who also brought suffering upon himself as he was ostracized because of his collusion with the Romans. Jesus restored him as a true son of Abraham (Luke 19).
- A man was crucified alongside Jesus. He was crucified because he was a thief and thus brought suffering on himself. Jesus forgave him and promised him a place in paradise (Luke 23:42–43).

Uncontrolled Circumstances

When persons suffered due to circumstances beyond their control, Jesus healed. He healed throughout His ministry:

> *Jesus went throughout Galilee, teaching in their synagogues, preaching the good news of the kingdom, and healing every disease and sickness among the people. News about him spread all over Syria, and people brought to him all who were ill with various diseases, those suffering severe pain, the demon-possessed, those having seizures, and the paralyzed, and he healed them.*
>
> **—Matthew 4:23–24**

There were occasions when Jesus raised some from the dead and brought comfort to their families:

- Jesus raised Jairus's daughter (Mark 5:21–24, 35–42)
- Jesus raised the widow's son (Luke 7:11–17)
- Jesus raised Lazarus (John 11:1–44)

Personal Obedience

Jesus set the example for His believers to follow in the circumstances where they suffer because of obedience to God's laws and kingdom standards. They (and we) were to entrust themselves to the One who "judges justly."

> When they hurled their insults at him, he did not retaliate; when he suffered, he made no threats. Instead, he entrusted himself to him who judges justly.
> —**1 Peter 2:23**

> If you suffer for doing good and you endure it, this is commendable before God. To this you were called, because Christ suffered for you, leaving you an example, that you should follow in his steps.
> —**1 Peter 2:20–21**

Jesus taught His followers:

> Blessed are those who are persecuted because of righteousness, for theirs is the kingdom of heaven. Blessed are you when people insult you, persecute you and falsely say all kinds of evil against you because of me. Rejoice and be glad, because great is your reward in heaven, for in the same way they persecuted the prophets who were before you.
> —**Matthew 5:10–12**

Thus, God's response to human suffering—whether caused by disobedience, obedience, or circumstances—is always to deliver, comfort, heal, restore, reconcile, forgive, and make whole.

God uses these opportunities to discipline, strengthen character, develop perseverance, and make us bold and confident in our faith. God never allows anything to go to waste.

We Have a Ministry to Comfort Others

As God has comforted us, we are called to comfort others. 2 Corinthians 1:3–5 says, "**so that** we can comfort those in any trouble with the comfort we ourselves have received from God" (authors' emphasis).

We are delivered, forgiven, comforted, restored, reconciled, and healed **so that** we may imitate our God as seen in Jesus Christ. "Be imitators of God, therefore, as dearly loved children and live a life of love, just as Christ loved us and gave himself up for us as a fragrant offering and sacrifice to God" (Eph. 5:1–2). Following His example, we become instruments of God's deliverance, forgiveness, comfort, restoration, reconciliation, and healing for others who experience the same needs as ourselves.

We are healed and made whole not merely for the sake of being healed and made whole; we are healed to be channels of healing for others.

Ministry is not optional for the Christian. It is a basic requirement as part of the body of Christ. Jesus instructed His disciples to "preach the kingdom of God and to heal the sick" (Luke 9 and 10).

That mandate has been part of the life of the church from the very beginning. Healing is the practical application of the Christian gospel.

We have now seen three affirmations about God. The first affirmation, then, is that God is our Comforter, not our afflicter. The second affirmation is that when we are afflicted, God comforts. The third affirmation is that God comforts so that we may comfort others.

IDEAS FOR REFLECTION

Please share at a level that is comfortable for you.

1. How have you received God's comfort when you have suffered as a result of disobedience, either because of Satan, others, or yourself?

2. How have you been comforted or blessed when you have suffered because you were obedient to the standards of the kingdom of God?

3. Share about those times when you have experienced God's forgiveness.

4. Share about those times when you have experienced God's healing touch.

5. Under what circumstances have you known that God was with you and provided healing for you?

6. When have you had opportunity to express gratitude to God for your own gift of His grace by ministering forgiveness, healing, and wholeness to another?

IV. THE HOLY SPIRIT— GOD'S PROMISED GIFT

This chapter focuses on the person and work of the Holy Spirit. A ministry of healing and wholeness finds its source of power in the person of the Holy Spirit. If ministry is to be effective and productive, then those in ministry must draw upon the supernatural power provided by God.

Jesus was anointed by the Holy Spirit and set apart for the ministry that He was called to do. He was empowered by God's Holy Spirit to accomplish that ministry, including the power to endure the cross.

It is that same Holy Spirit who anoints, sets apart, and empowers us, the people of God, to do the work God calls us to do.

SCRIPTURE:

Wait for the gift my Father promised, which you have heard me speak about. For John baptized with water, but in a few days you will be baptized with the Holy Spirit. . . . you will receive power when the Holy Spirit comes on you; and you will be my witnesses . . . to the ends of the earth.

—Acts 1:4–5, 8

When Jesus was preparing to leave His disciples at the time of His ascension into heaven, He told them, "I am going to send you what my Father has promised; but stay in the city until you have been clothed with power from on high" (Luke 24:49).

Jesus was telling the disciples that God had promised the Holy Spirit through the ages, and it was now time for that promise to be fulfilled for the purpose of empowering them for ministry in and to the world. God's promised gift is His Holy Spirit.

Throughout Israel's history, God spoke through the prophets to let the people know that God's Spirit would be upon them. Through the prophet Isaiah, God said, "I will pour out my Spirit on your offspring, and my blessing on your descendants" (44:3). Later, through the prophet Ezekiel, God repeated the promise: "I will put my Spirit in you and move you to follow my decrees and be careful to keep my laws" (36:27).

It appears that originally the promise was intended for the nation of Israel, the people who had been chosen to display to the world God's grace, mercy, and power. Through the prophet Joel, God expanded the boundaries of that promise.

Joel prophesied a new dimension to God's promise: "I will pour out my Spirit on **all** people. Your sons and daughters will prophesy, your old men will dream dreams, your young men will see visions. Even on my servants, both men and women, I will pour out my Spirit in those days" (2:28–29, authors' emphasis).

It was not that God's Spirit had been inactive among God's people. During the time of the old covenant, the Holy Spirit had empowered prophets, priests, and kings for the work that God had called them to do. When they were obedient to God's call and command, the Spirit remained and their work succeeded. When they were disobedient, the Spirit was removed and their position of responsibility and power quickly came to an end.

God's promise of the Holy Spirit was fulfilled in the life of Jesus when He was baptized in the Jordan River and the Spirit came upon Him in the form of a dove (Luke 3:21–22). The Spirit of God, which was given and rescinded intermittently under the old covenant, was poured out on Jesus—Prophet, Priest, and King—never to be removed again. In Him, all the fullness of God is pleased to dwell—always (Col. 1:19).

Jesus, God's anointed One, came to fulfill the promise of the Holy Spirit to the world. The Holy Spirit who descended upon Him and remained was also to come and remain upon His followers.

That promise was fulfilled in the life of the disciples on Pentecost when the Holy Spirit was poured out on those gathered in the Upper Room in Jerusalem (Acts 2). The Holy Spirit, God's promised gift, came upon the disciples, never to leave.

In the following pages, five questions will be asked relative to the person and work of the Holy Spirit. The remainder of this chapter will focus on the first two of these questions and the next chapter will consider the final three:

- Who is the Holy Spirit?
- What is the work of the Holy Spirit?
- What does it mean to be baptized with the Holy Spirit?
- What happens when a person is baptized with the Holy Spirit?
- How may a person be baptized with the Holy Spirit?

Who Is the Holy Spirit?

The Holy Spirit is the third person in the triune Godhead: God, the Father; God, the Son; God, the Holy Spirit. The Holy Spirit is *not* a third god, nor one-third of God. The Holy Spirit *is* God's living presence in our midst and in our lives. The Holy Spirit is the indwelling presence of the risen and living Christ.

The Holy Spirit is the Spirit of the Holy God perfectly revealed in Jesus who is God incarnate in the flesh. As we know, the word incarnate means to be given form—that which is abstract is made real. God, who is Spirit, is given form in Jesus. Jesus told His disciples, "Anyone who has seen me has seen the Father" (John 14:9).

In order to understand the nature of the Holy Spirit, we must understand that which we can of the nature of God. We gain that understanding from Scripture. Much about God's nature we cannot understand. How can the finite mind comprehend the infinite? How can that which knows in part understand that which is whole? How can that which is mortal understand that which is eternal? How can that which is imperfect comprehend perfection? Some things remain a mystery.

Nevertheless, God has chosen to reveal much of that divine nature through Jesus, the Word become flesh, and through the Scriptures, the written Word of God. With the help of Scripture and the guidance of the Holy Spirit, we can come to know something of the nature of God and thus the nature of God's Holy Spirit.

The following scriptural insights into the nature of God were discussed in chapter 1:

- God is holy (Lev. 11:45; 1 Pet. 1:15)
- God is spirit (John 4:24)
- God is a consuming fire (Heb. 12:29)
- God is light (1 John 1:5)
- God is love (1 John 4:16)

Additionally, **God is person**. Scripture reveals throughout that God is person, not in the sense that you and I are persons, but in the sense that God has personality. God shows compassion, comfort, mercy, grace, kindness, patience, justice, wisdom, peace, joy, wrath, anger, faithfulness, and steadfastness. These and many other traits are associated with personality.

As person, God responds to our human condition with heart, that is, with feeling. God feels our pain and our hurt. God also feels our joy and our rejoicing. God grieves over our rebellion and our sin. God rejoices over our obedience and our worship.

The Holy Spirit is the Spirit of the Holy God of Creation, through whom worlds were spoken into being. The Holy Spirit is the Spirit of the God of Adam and Eve, of Abraham and Sarah, of Isaac and Rebekah, of Jacob and Rachel, of Moses and Miriam, of Saul, David, Solomon, Elijah, Esther, Isaiah, Joel, Jeremiah, Ruth, and all the other women and men of old and new covenant times who responded to God's declaration, "I will walk among you and be your God, and you shall be My people" (Lev. 26:12 NKJV).

The Holy Spirit is the Spirit of the all-consuming God who touched and purified the lives of prophets, priests, and kings, inspiring them to do that which was in harmony with God's will and which would bring life to God's people.

The Holy Spirit is the Spirit of the enlightening God who was made perfectly known in Jesus the Christ—the Word become flesh—the living and visible presence of the invisible and eternal Spirit.

The Holy Spirit is the Spirit of the empowering God who poured Himself into Peter, James, John, and all the other disciples at Pentecost, enabling them to spread the gospel to the ends of the earth.

The Holy Spirit is the Spirit of the teacher God who taught the disciples; who witnessed about Jesus; who convicted people of guilt in regard to sin, righteousness, and judgment; who guided people into truth; who counseled, encouraged, and comforted people; who revealed God's will to people; who gave people freedom and guaranteed them eternal life.

The Holy Spirit is the Spirit of the loving God who immersed that early band of believers in powerful love that enabled them to love the world as God did. They were empowered to proclaim that love as God in Christ proclaimed it. They were willing to die for humankind that it may experience that love, following the example of Jesus who gave His life that the world may live eternally in that love.

The Holy Spirit is the Spirit of the Holy God who is perfectly revealed in Jesus, who is holiness, spirit, consuming fire, power, authority, light, and love incarnate in the flesh.

If we desire to understand the nature of God and God's Spirit, we have only to look at the life of Jesus Christ who is the Light that enlightens all people, for Jesus is "the radiance of God's glory and the exact representation of his being" (Heb. 1:3). His life is the glory (essence/substance) of God and, as Jesus told Philip, when we see Jesus, we see the Father (John 14:9).

What Is the Work of the Holy Spirit?

Jesus spent considerable time teaching the disciples about the Holy Spirit and what the Holy Spirit would be doing in and through their lives. He taught them about the person and work of the Holy Spirit and reminded them of that on the day of His ascension into heaven. His teachings are summarized in chapters fourteen, fifteen, and sixteen of the Gospel of John.

Paraclete

> *"I will ask the Father, and he will give you another Counselor [Paraclete] to be with you forever . . ."*
>
> —**John 14:16**

The Greek word *paraclete* is variously translated into English as counselor, comforter, encourager, advocate. The Holy Spirit is to be seen as continuing the same work in which Jesus was involved as He walked among the disciples. Certainly Jesus was the Counselor, the Comforter, the Encourager, and the Advocate. Likewise, that is the work of the Holy Spirit. The Paraclete is the One who comes alongside with strength and helps.

Teacher

Jesus also taught that the Holy Spirit is the Teacher. "The Counselor, the Holy Spirit, whom the Father will send in my name, will teach you all things and will remind you of everything I have said to you" (John 14:26).

The early church depended upon the Holy Spirit to teach them and to remind them of what Jesus had taught. The very record of Scripture is one of the greatest evidences of this work of the Holy Spirit, as persons were inspired by the Spirit to write down what they remembered Jesus saying and doing.

The apostle John later reemphasizes this to the early church when he wrote in his first epistle, "But the anointing which you have received from Him abides in you, and you do not need that anyone teach you; but as the same anointing teaches you concerning all things, and is true, and is not a lie, and just as it has taught you, you will abide in Him" (2:27 NKJV).

Counselor-Advisor

The work of the Holy Spirit is to be Counselor in the sense that Luke and Mark tell about in their gospels.

> *Settle it therefore in your minds, not to meditate beforehand how to answer; for I will give you a mouth and wisdom, which none of your adversaries will be able to withstand or contradict.*
>
> —**Luke 21:14–15** RSV

And when they bring you to trial and deliver you up, do not be anxious beforehand what you are to say; but say whatever is given you in that hour, for it is not you who speak, but the Holy Spirit.

—Mark 13:11 RSV

Spirit of Truth

As the Spirit of Truth, it is the work of the Holy Spirit to lead humanity into all truth, especially as it relates to the nature of God as revealed in Jesus Christ. In John 16:13, Jesus declared that the Spirit of Truth will guide us into all truth. In John 17:17, Jesus defines truth as God's Word: "Thy Word is Truth" (KJV).

If you love me, you will keep my commandments. And I will pray the Father, and he will give you another Counselor, to be with you for ever, even the Spirit of truth, whom the world cannot receive, because it neither sees him nor knows him; you know him, for he dwells with you, and will be in you.

—John 14:15–17 RSV

Witness to Testify

A witness testifies in court as to what was seen and heard and tells the truth. Jesus said that the Son could do and say only what He heard the Father doing and saying (John 5:19, 12:50). The work of the Holy Spirit is to bring us to focus on Jesus in the same way. The Holy Spirit leads us to do what we see Jesus doing and speak the truth of what we hear Jesus saying.

Jesus is the focal point of the Holy Spirit's ministry. All that the Holy Spirit does reveals Jesus and sets an example for the followers of Jesus to emulate. All that Jesus did pointed to God and all that the Holy Spirit does points to Jesus.

When the Counselor comes, whom I will send to you from the Father, the Spirit of truth who goes out from the Father, he will testify about me. And you also must testify, for you have been with me from the beginning.

—John 15:26–27

Just as the Holy Spirit testifies about Jesus, so Jesus testifies—bears witness—to God.

I tell you the truth, the Son can do nothing by himself; he can do only what he sees his Father doing, because whatever the Father does the Son also does. For the Father loves the Son and shows him all he does.

—John 5:19–20

For I did not speak of my own accord, but the Father who sent me commanded me what to say and how to say it. I know that his command leads to eternal life. So whatever I say is just what the Father has told me to say.

—John 12:49–50

Convicter

Jesus told the disciples:

When he [Holy Spirit] comes, he will convict the world of guilt in regard to sin and righteousness and judgment: in regard to sin, because men do not believe in me; in regard to righteousness, because I am going to the Father, where you can see me no longer; and in regard to judgment, because the prince of this world now stands condemned.

—**John 16:8–11**

Only God understands the nature and consequences of sin and of righteousness and of judgment. Therefore, only God's Spirit is in a position to bring conviction relative to these. Such conviction of guilt and passing of judgment are not left in the hands of imperfect people, but are reserved for God's Spirit alone.

Guide

A guide is one who goes on ahead, scouts out the terrain, and provides leadership to the determined destination. In the kingdom of God, God's truth is the destination and the Spirit leads us through the various peripheral issues until truth is revealed.

. . . when he, the Spirit of truth, comes, he will guide you into all truth.

—**John 16:13**

Revealer

The work of the Holy Spirit is to reveal to God's people what is yet to come, thereby preparing us ahead of time for what is yet to be.

. . . he will tell you what is yet to come. He will bring glory to me by taking from what is mine and making it known to you.

—**John 16:13b–14**

The apostle Paul is led by the Lord to reveal in his writings other facets of the nature of the Holy Spirit and reminds the church of other works of the Holy Spirit. These are certainly in harmony with the teachings of Jesus.

Giver of Freedom

Paul came to understand that the Holy Spirit is the source and giver of freedom.

Now the Lord is the Spirit, and where the Spirit of the Lord is, there is freedom. . . . [this] comes from the Lord, who is the Spirit.

—**2 Corinthians 3:17–18**

When we are alienated from God, we are in bondage to that which is not of God. We are in bondage to sin or, as Jesus stated in John's Gospel, "Everyone who sins is a slave to sin" (8:34). The apostle Paul declares in his letter to the Romans, "You have been set free from sin and have become slaves to righteousness" (Rom. 6:18). And to the Galatians he declared, "It is for freedom that Christ has set us free" (Gal. 5:1).

The Holy Spirit, the Spirit of the Resurrected Christ, sets us free from sin and its consequences and brings us into freedom to walk in a reconciled relationship with God.

Guarantor of Our Inheritance

The Holy Spirit is the One with whom we are sealed for the day of redemption and is the One who guarantees our inheritance.

> *Having believed, you were marked in him with a seal, the promised Holy Spirit, who is a deposit guaranteeing our inheritance until the redemption of those who are God's possession.*
> **—Ephesians 1:13–14**

Revelation of the work of the Holy Spirit did not end with the early Christians. Charles Wesley, though most noted for his many great hymns, was like his brother John, a very gifted preacher. The following are points from one of Charles Wesley's sermons entitled, "Awake Thou That Sleepest."

- By faith we receive the Holy Spirit which is of God to replace the spirit of the world which is in us. The Holy Spirit, Christ in us, is the greatest gift God has promised to man.

- We are called to be a habitation of God through His Holy Spirit. Through His Holy Spirit dwelling in us, we are to be saints here and partakers of the inheritance of the saints of light.

- The antichrist denies the indwelling Holy Spirit is the privilege of all believers. The antichrist denies this blessing of the Gospel, this unspeakable gift, this universal promise, this criterion of a real Christian.

- The Church teaches us to pray for the inspiration of the Holy Spirit. We are taught to pray that we may be filled with the Holy Spirit. Every presbyter of the Church claims to have received the Holy Spirit by the laying on of hands at ordination.

- As of old, this belief in the Holy Spirit is almost universally denied, ridiculed and exploded as mere frenzy or fad. Those who believe it are still branded as madmen or fanatics.

The work of the Holy Spirit is the completion of the work that was begun by Jesus. The Holy Spirit is Counselor, Comforter, Encourager, Advocate, and Friend. The Holy Spirit is the Spirit of Truth who guides into all truth. The Holy Spirit is Teacher, Witness, Convicter, Revealer, the Giver of Freedom, and the Guarantor of our Inheritance until we acquire possession of it.

Who is the Holy Spirit? The Holy Spirit is God's promised gift, the fulfillment of which promise was accomplished in the life, death, and resurrection of Jesus Christ.

IDEAS FOR REFLECTION

Please share at a level that is comfortable for you.

1. Discuss the statement, "The Holy Spirit is not a third god, nor is the Holy Spirit one-third of God. The Holy Spirit is God."

2. Discuss the statement, "The Holy Spirit is the Spirit of the Holy God who is revealed in Jesus, who is God incarnate in the flesh."

3. One work of the Holy Spirit is to anoint, set apart, and empower believers for ministry. What has the Holy Spirit anointed you to do?

V. BAPTISM AND THE HOLY SPIRIT

Now we will focus on the remaining three questions relative to Jesus' statement to the disciples that they would be baptized with the Holy Spirit.

SCRIPTURE:

For John baptized with water, but in a few days you will be baptized with the Holy Spirit.

—Acts 1:5

What Does It Mean to Be Baptized with the Holy Spirit?

Water Baptism

When the apostle Paul asked the Ephesian elders what baptism they received, they replied, "John's baptism." Paul said, "John's baptism was a baptism of repentance. He told the people to believe in the one coming after him, that is, in Jesus" (Acts 19:3–4).

Water baptism for the Christian symbolizes dying to the old self, being washed clean, being raised to new life, and being incorporated into the body of Christ.

The apostle Paul writes in his letter to the Colossians, "having been buried with him [Jesus] in baptism and raised with him through your faith in the power of God, who raised him from the dead" (2:12).

Spirit Baptism

However, Jesus said that the disciples would be baptized, not with water, but with the Holy Spirit. Since the Holy Spirit is the Spirit of the Holy God and "baptize" means to immerse, to be baptized with the Holy Spirit is to be immersed in God's nature. In other words, to be baptized in the Holy Spirit is to be immersed in God's holiness, God's Spirit, God's consuming fire, God's light, God's love, and God's own person.

John's baptism was a baptism in water for repentance. Jesus' baptism is a baptism with the Holy Spirit for empowerment.

What Happens When You Are Baptized with the Holy Spirit?

What happens to us as a result of being baptized with the Holy Spirit must be seen in light of all the work that the Spirit accomplishes in our lives. Baptism with the Holy Spirit is not a move of the Spirit apart from other moves of God's Spirit and must be understood as part of God's total work in our lives.

Before the first disciples experienced that which Jesus had told them would happen at Pentecost (namely, that they would be baptized with the Holy Spirit), the Spirit had already been working in their lives through the life of Jesus. Likewise, the Holy Spirit is at work in the pre-Pentecost days of our lives as well as on the day of Pentecost and the days after.

The early disciples had already been drawn into a right relationship with God through Jesus Christ. Their lives were already being transformed by God's presence for at least three years before the outpouring of the Holy Spirit at Pentecost. Pentecost opened the door for a new and more powerful relationship with God than they had known before, but God had prepared them for it.

Justification

One result of the work of the Holy Spirit is that we come to understand the meaning of our justification, the fact that we are born again. Justification by faith and the forgiveness of sin brings about the healing of our spirit in our relationship with God. We are no longer alienated from the Source of our lives. It is "just-as-if-I'd" never sinned.

In the Wesleyan tradition, we believe that God's Spirit is always wooing us and endeavoring to draw us into a right relationship with God even before we are aware of it. While we are still dead in our sins, the Spirit of God moves to bring us to salvation and life. "But God demonstrates His own love toward us, in that while we were still sinners, Christ died for us" (Rom. 5:8 NKJV).

This work of God's grace we call **prevenient grace**—the grace that goes before. It is the grace of God that is at work even before we know it and brings us to the place where we can be reconciled with God. Grace is God's unmerited favor. It is prevenient grace that brings us to the point in our lives where we can say yes to Jesus and come to know God's justifying grace when we are made right with God.

Jesus told Nicodemus, "unless one is born of water and the Spirit, he cannot enter the kingdom of God. That which is born of the flesh is flesh, and that which is born of the Spirit is spirit" (John 3:5–6 RSV). We are born of the flesh in the natural human birth process, and consequently, we are flesh—mortal flesh.

When Christ Jesus enters our lives, His Holy Spirit takes up residence there, for where Christ is, there is the Holy Spirit. It is the Holy Spirit who gives us spiritual birth. It is then that we are born of the Spirit: "But you are not in the flesh, you are in the Spirit, if in fact the Spirit of God dwells in you. Any one who does not have the Spirit of Christ does not belong to him" (Rom. 8:9 RSV).

Sanctification

A second result of the work of the Holy Spirit is that the Spirit begins the work of sanctification (in the Greek and Hebrew, "to be set apart, to be made holy"). In other words, the Holy Spirit cleans up our lives.

> But when the kindness and love of God our Savior appeared, he saved us, not because of righteous things we had done, but because of his mercy. He saved us through the washing of rebirth and renewal by the Holy Spirit, whom he poured out on us generously through Jesus

Christ our Savior, so that, having been justified by his grace, we might become heirs having the hope of eternal life.

—Titus 3:4–5

This is sanctifying grace—the grace that begins to change our lives, to make us holy, and to set us apart for royal use within the kingdom of God. It is, as Charles Wesley said in his sermon, "the Holy Spirit who replaces the spirit of the world that is in us."

John Wesley's sermon titled "The New Birth" shows the relationship between our new birth and the sanctifying work of the Holy Spirit.

When we are born again, then our sanctification, our inward and outward holiness, begins; and thenceforward we are gradually to "grow up in Him who is our Head." This expression of the Apostle admirably illustrates the difference between one and the other, and farther points out the exact analogy there is between natural and spiritual things. A child is born of a woman in a moment, or at least in a very short time: Afterward he gradually and slowly grows, till he attains to the stature of a man. In like manner, a child is born of God in a short time, if not in a moment. But it is by slow degrees that he afterward grows up to the measure of the full stature of Christ. The same relation, therefore, which there is between our natural birth and our growth, there is also between our new birth and our sanctification.

Justification is what God does *for* us. Sanctification is what God does *in* us.

Fruit of the Spirit

A third result of the work of the Holy Spirit is the development of the fruit of God's own nature—the fruit of the Spirit in our lives. As the fruit of the Spirit grows in our lives, the Holy Spirit's nature becomes our nature—not through our own efforts or works but through the Spirit's presence dwelling within us (indwelling presence).

The fruit of the Spirit has to do with who we are in Christ. Whereas justification is what God does *for* us and sanctification is what God does *in* us, the fruit of the Spirit is what God does *to* us. People who are baptized with the Holy Spirit are known by the spiritual fruit in their lives.

The apostle Paul, inspired by the Spirit of God, wrote that "The fruit of the Spirit is love, joy, peace, patience, kindness, goodness, faithfulness, gentleness and self-control" (Gal. 5:22–23).

All this is the work of the Holy Spirit in our lives, even from the time when God knit us together in our mother's womb (Ps. 139:13) to the present.

Release of Empowering Gifts

When we are baptized with the Holy Spirit, we are empowered for ministry. As Jesus told His disciples, "And behold, I send the promise of my Father upon you; but stay in the city, until you are clothed with power from on high" (Luke 24:49 RSV). He also told them on the day of His ascension, "But you will receive power when the Holy Spirit comes on you; and you will be my witnesses" (Acts 1:8).

When the apostle Paul wrote to the Christians in Corinth, he said, "my speech and my message were not in plausible words of wisdom, but in demonstration of the Spirit and of power, that your faith might not rest in the wisdom of men but in the power of God" (1 Cor. 2:4–5 RSV).

The Lord assigns a task and then He gives the spiritual gifts (spiritual tools) necessary to accomplish that task. We are called to preach the gospel and heal the sick. God empowers us to do just that through the indwelling presence and power of the Holy Spirit and the spiritual gifts.

The spiritual gifts of knowledge, wisdom, discernment of spirits, prophecy, tongues, interpretation of tongues, faith, miracles, and gifts of healing are all powerful manifestations of the Holy Spirit in the lives of those who are called and empowered for ministry (1 Cor. 12:1–11).

These are the spiritual gifts with which we are empowered to do the work God calls us to do. When we are baptized with the Holy Spirit, the power of the Spirit is released in us to preach the gospel, heal the sick, forgive sins, drive out demons, and make disciples for our Lord Jesus Christ.

> *Then the disciples went out and preached everywhere, and the Lord worked with them and confirmed his word by the signs that accompanied it.*
>
> —Mark 16:20

How May I Be Baptized with the Holy Spirit?

The way by which we may be baptized with the Holy Spirit is to ask Jesus to baptize us with the Holy Spirit. That is the direction and assurance given in Holy Scripture. Jesus said:

> *And I tell you, Ask, and it will be given you; seek, and you will find; knock, and it will be opened to you. For every one who asks receives, and he who seeks finds, and to him who knocks it will be opened. What father among you, if his son asks for a fish, will instead of a fish give him a serpent; or if he asks for an egg, will give him a scorpion? If you then, who are evil, know how to give good gifts to your children, how much more will the heavenly Father give the Holy Spirit to those who ask him!*
>
> —Luke 11:9–13 RSV

The twelve disciples did not ask to be baptized with the Holy Spirit. Jesus had instructed them that in a few days they would receive the gift that God had promised. They were most likely aware of who the Holy Spirit was because Jesus had taught them. However, as to what it meant to be baptized with the Holy Spirit, they were probably not aware. In the meantime, they did as Jesus had instructed. They waited in the Upper Room in Jerusalem, entered into worship and prayer, and anticipated the gift that God had promised and about which Jesus had spoken. Then, they were all filled with the Holy Spirit (Acts 2:4).

In describing to the people what had happened, the apostle Peter said, "Exalted to the right hand of God, he [Jesus] has received from the Father the promised Holy Spirit and has poured out what you now see and hear" (Acts 2:33). The disciples had not asked. It happened as Jesus had said.

Since that time, the scriptural way in which we may be baptized with the Holy Spirit is by asking.

How may I be baptized with the Holy Spirit? *Ask!*

A Process by which We May Be Baptized with the Holy Spirit

Please understand that, as with any process, the process itself is not what brings about baptism with the Holy Spirit. Jesus is the Baptizer and may use any process to bring about that which He desires to happen. At the same time, we have a part in it and that is to be open to allowing Jesus to baptize us with His Holy Spirit.

1. First, our life needs to be committed to Jesus Christ as our Savior and Lord. This is true for longtime believers and new believers.

2. Next, we ask Jesus to baptize us with the Holy Spirit. Then we believe that He is faithful to do that which has been promised. We ask for and expect a release of the power of the Holy Spirit in our lives.

3. Then, we thank God for the gift of the Holy Spirit—the giving of which is based on God's faithfulness to God's Word and not on our feelings. It does not matter if we do not feel any emotional response or change in our physical posture. Belief that we have been baptized in the Holy Spirit is based on God always keeping His promises.

4. Since we can trust in God's faithfulness to fulfill the promise of God's Word, we then witness to the presence of God's Holy Spirit by telling someone about it. We confess with our lips that God has indeed poured out the Holy Spirit into our lives.

5. We anticipate that the Holy Spirit will be manifested in our lives through one or more of the supernatural gifts that empower us for ministry. We, like the disciples at Pentecost, the Ephesian elders, or the Gentiles in Caesarea, may prophesy and/or speak in tongues when the Holy Spirit is released in our lives. Other gifts and manifestations of the Spirit may also become evident as the Holy Spirit begins to do His work.

6. As we learn to walk in the Spirit and obey the Spirit, we allow the Holy Spirit to mature us and grow us up in the fullness of Jesus Christ, for that is God's ultimate aim for our lives—to be like Jesus. That is accomplished through the person and work of the Holy Spirit.

God is faithful to His word. If we ask to be baptized with the Holy Spirit, then God will pour out His Holy Spirit upon us, filling us with the power about which Jesus told His disciples (Acts 1:8) and equipping us for the ministry to which God graciously calls us.

IDEAS FOR REFLECTION

Please share at a level that is comfortable for you.

1. Take time to discuss questions related to the work of the Holy Spirit and what it means to be baptized with the Holy Spirit.

2. When all have had opportunity to discuss questions about the person and work of the Holy Spirit, invite those individuals in the group who desire, to pray together the following closing prayer:

Prayer:

"Gracious and loving God, I come before You to confess my sins. I name them in my heart. [Here, take time to silently name those things that the Holy Spirit brings to your mind that need to be confessed.] I ask You to forgive me. [Here, take time to experience God's forgiveness.] I thank You for Your forgiveness.

"Jesus, I believe in You. I believe in Your life, death, and resurrection. I believe that You died for me. I believe that Your blood covers all my sins. I ask You to come into my heart. Live in me and be the Savior and Lord of my life.

"Jesus, I ask You to baptize me with Your Holy Spirit. Fill me with Your eternal love so that I may be totally Yours—spirit, soul, and body. My desire is to be the temple of Your Holy Spirit. I give the Holy Spirit permission to be released in my life.

"Holy Spirit, be my Teacher, my Counselor, my Guide, my Comforter, my Friend. Guard my steps that I may walk in the footsteps of Jesus. Empower me to share my faith with others that they too may come to know Jesus Christ as their Lord and Savior. It is in His name I pray. Amen."

VI. THE WORD OF KNOWLEDGE

This chapter focuses on one of the primary and most vital spiritual gifts used on a regular basis in the ministry of healing and wholeness—the gift of the word of knowledge. Through the use of this gift, God provides direction for accomplishing what He desires when we are given a ministry task.

SCRIPTURE:

Now to each one the manifestation of the Spirit is given for the common good. To one there is given through the Spirit the message of wisdom, to another the message of knowledge by means of the same Spirit, to another faith by the same Spirit, to another gifts of healings by that one Spirit, to another miraculous powers, to another prophecy, to another distinguishing between spirits, to another speaking in different kinds of tongues, and to still another the interpretation of tongues. All these are the work of one and the same Spirit, and he gives them to each one, just as he determines.

—1 Corinthians 12:7–11

When the apostle Paul wrote to the Christian church in Corinth, he said, "Now about spiritual gifts, brothers, I do not want you to be ignorant [or uninformed]" (1 Cor. 12:1). He desired that the Corinthian Christians be aware of spiritual gifts and be knowledgeable about them. The apostle Paul wanted the early followers to know what these gifts were, where they came from, and how they were used in the ministry of Christ's church.

Different Types of Gifts

Spiritual Gifts

A spiritual gift finds its source in the Holy Spirit. It is a supernatural gift from God designed by Him to be used in the ministry of His kingdom. God intends for the ministry of Christ's church to be accomplished by the power of the Holy Spirit and the spiritual gifts that are manifested (shown) in and through the lives of believers.

Talents

A talent is not the same as a spiritual gift. A natural talent is a grace given by God to all people, believers and unbelievers alike, that enables people to live and function in the human society.

Persons may have a natural ability or talent to do certain things that enable them to function without acknowledging that it came from God or seeking God's help in using it. For example, there are highly talented singers, teachers, actors, leaders, speakers, and others who work hard, drawing on all the natural talent that they have, but who are not spiritually empowered or gifted.

A natural talent can function apart from any acknowledgment of God's help, whereas spiritual gifts cannot function apart from the empowering presence of God's Holy Spirit.

Professional Tools

Every work and profession has tools used to accomplish that particular line of work. Teachers, engineers, housewives, artists, architects, keyboard operators, nurses, secretaries, firemen, policemen, models, athletes, and others perform their work by the employment of certain tools related to their work.

For example, the teacher uses pens, books, chalkboards, and paper to accomplish his or her work. Others use hammers, brushes, pots and pans, computers, thermometers, microscopes, brooms, and many other tools for their trade.

If tools are essential for doing our secular work, how much more so are the spiritual tools necessary to accomplish God's work in His kingdom?

The spiritual gifts, or spiritual tools, that God gives to be used for ministry are absolutely essential if we, the church, are to accomplish what God has called us to do.

- How do we know right from wrong in this world without using the gift of discernment?

- How does our spirit pray "in the Spirit" without the gift of tongues and the interpretation of tongues?

- How can we preach the gospel without the gifts of knowledge, wisdom, and prophecy?

- How can we heal the sick without using the gifts of faith, miracles, and healing?

The word of knowledge is one spiritual tool that is essential in the ministry of healing and wholeness. Through its use, we come to know what God desires to accomplish in a given situation.

Through the prophet Jeremiah, God told us, "Call to me and I will answer you and tell you great and unsearchable things you do not know" (33:3). Those great and unsearchable things that we do not and could not possibly know, unless God chooses to reveal them to us, are God's words of knowledge.

Kinds of Knowledge

Natural Knowledge

All of us have natural knowledge. It is what we learn from the time we are born. It ranges from the very basics of learning to eat, to speak, and to walk, to whatever level of our intellect we allow to be developed through schooling or our profession.

Natural knowledge is important to our well-being in this world. It enables effective communication, positive social relationships, personal achievements, productive living, and fulfilling accomplishments. However, **natural knowledge has limitations,** such as:

- Some of the things we learn today will become obsolete tomorrow. We live in an age where knowledge increases on a daily basis and systems that were futuristic yesterday are history tomorrow. We live in an age of science. It is a relatively new era, for here at the beginning of the twenty-first century, most of the scientists who have ever lived are still alive.

- Research brings new discoveries in the field of medicine almost every day. While we are learning new things today, we are unlearning things that we learned yesterday, for those things have become obsolete. Many of the tools that were used in acquiring our new knowledge for yesterday have been replaced by tools that are newer and more effective.

- Another problem that can develop with natural knowledge is that we can become so reliant on our natural knowledge, we fail to even ask God for answers. Since we know how something is to be done or accomplished, there is no need to seek divine help or direction.

- One consequence of this self-reliant attitude is that we can become prideful with our knowledge. Scripture reminds us that "knowledge puffs up" (1 Cor. 8:1). Pride will separate us from God and from people.

- Another consequence of relying on our own knowldege is that since we live in an era when natural knowledge is rapidly changing, the day will most likely come when we find ourselves in an unfamiliar environment where we know neither the subject nor the answer and our natural knowledge fails us completely.

- Natural knowledge is not adequate for the work of the supernatural kingdom, especially in the area of healing and wholeness. It is imperative that Christians draw on knowledge that goes beyond the level of natural knowledge.

Eternal Knowledge

Eternal knowledge is knowledge that brings us to see and understand the things of this world from God's perspective. Eternal knowledge comes as we allow God's Holy Spirit to teach us about the kingdom of God. Scripture reminds us that the Holy Spirit is our Teacher and "he will teach you all things, and bring to your remembrance all that I [Jesus] have said to you" (John 14:26 RSV).

As the Holy Spirit teaches us, we begin to take on "the mind of Christ" (1 Cor. 2:16). As we do this, we learn how to think as God thinks, will what God wills, and do what God does. Jesus prayed that God would sanctify us in truth and that God's Word is truth (John 17:17). We grow in eternal knowledge as the Spirit teaches us the truth of God's Word.

Eternal knowledge brings us to the place of knowing more of God and the ways of God. It teaches us how to live by kingdom principles and standards that are unchanging. Therefore, unlike natural knowledge, eternal knowledge does not become obsolete tomorrow. Our understanding of God's Word changes from day to day, but the truth of God's Word never changes.

When the Holy Spirit teaches us the truth of God's Word, we cannot be proud, for we know that the truth revealed to us has come from the Spirit and not from our own ingenuity or thinking processes.

As we receive Jesus Christ into our hearts, we allow our minds to be changed into His likeness, and allow the Holy Spirit to teach us the truth of God's Word. We grow in eternal knowledge. That growth is a lifelong learning process.

Word of Knowledge

God's word of knowledge, however, is neither natural nor eternal knowledge, important as they are. The word of knowledge is not a result of ability, learning, or training. The word of knowledge comes in a situation where it is not humanly possible to know the answer and God gives direction in an instant on how to meet a human need.

Word of knowledge is given for direction, correction, encouragement, and understanding. It is given to reveal a need and how that need may be met according to God's desire and will. It is given to reveal what is in the heart of people so that healing may happen and they be drawn into a closer relationship with God.

In the ministry of healing and wholeness, God gives the word of knowledge so those who are in ministry may know what God desires to have done or be revealed in that given situation. It allows those in ministry to do as Jesus did, "I only do what I see my Father doing" (John 5:19, paraphrased). The word of knowledge allows us to see with the eyes of faith as God speaks to our hearts the answer that is needed for the human problem.

Jesus used this spiritual gift in His ministry. On one occasion, He was talking with a Samaritan woman at a well near the village of Sychar. It was noontime, the heat of the day. In their conversation Jesus said, "Go and call your husband." She replied, "I have no husband." Jesus said, "You have spoken correctly. You have had five husbands and the one you have now is not yours" (John 4:16–18, paraphrased).

The woman ran back to the village and told the people to come and see the man who told her all about her life. Could he possibly be the Christ? The people came and listened to His message and many believed. The villagers came to listen to Jesus because of what He had told the woman about her marital status.

Jesus did not personally know the woman, so how could He know about her relationships? He knew because He exercised the spiritual gift of the word of knowledge. The Holy Spirit revealed to Jesus the condition of this woman's heart and life. And, as becomes obvious in the rest of the story, it was done to draw her and the village into a greater understanding and acceptance of God.

The truth of God's Word is validated: "So is my word that goes out from my mouth: It will not return to me empty, but will accomplish what I desire and achieve the purpose for which I sent it" (Isa. 55:11).

On another occasion, Jesus was talking with His disciples near Caesarea Philippi. Jesus asked:

> *"Who do people say the Son of Man is?" They replied, "Some say John the Baptist; others say Elijah; and still others, Jeremiah or one of the prophets." "But what about you?" he asked. "Who do you say I am?" Simon Peter answered, "You are the Christ, the Son of the living God." Jesus replied, "Blessed are you, Simon son of Jonah, for this was not revealed to you by man, but by my Father in heaven."*
>
> —Matthew 16:13–17

Peter could not know that Jesus was God's Son unless God chose to reveal it to him. God's word of knowledge reveals truth and accomplishes the purpose for which God sends it.

God Speaks in Many Ways

Audible Voice

God has always spoken to people. He spoke to Moses through a burning bush that was not consumed. When Moses investigated the bush, he heard God call his name in an audible voice and tell him to take off his shoes for he was standing on holy ground (Exod. 3:4–5). God told Moses he was to leave his sheep and go back to Egypt and lead the Israelites out of captivity. God continued to speak to Moses through an audible voice as Moses led the people of Israel out of slavery into the wilderness and toward the Promised Land.

God spoke to Jesus with an audible voice. When John baptized Jesus in the Jordan River, God said, "This is my beloved Son, with whom I am well pleased" (Matt. 3:17 RSV).

On the Mount of Transfiguration the disciples heard God say, "This is my Son, whom I love; with him I am well pleased. Listen to him!" (Matt. 17:5).

Does God still speak in an audible voice today? Yes. The word of the prophet Isaiah is as contemporary as the day on which it was spoken, "Whether you turn to the right or to the left, your ears will hear a voice behind you, saying, 'This is the way; walk in it'" (Isa. 30:21). Therefore, you may hear God speak to you in an audible voice. Be aware, however, that others with you may or may not hear the audible voice that is so clear to you.

Scripture

Quite often God speaks to us through Scripture. "All Scripture is God-breathed and is useful for teaching, rebuking, correcting and training in righteousness, so that the man of God may be thoroughly equipped for every good work" (2 Tim. 3:16–17).

When Jesus was led by the Holy Spirit into the wilderness, He was tempted by the devil.

> *The tempter came to him and said, "If you are the Son of God, tell these stones to become bread." Jesus answered, "It is written: 'Man does not live on bread alone, but on every word that comes from the mouth of God.'"*
>
> **—Matthew 4:3–4**

In this, and the other temptations, Jesus could have turned the stones into bread. He could have had the angels catch Him had He thrown himself from the temple. He could have received all the kingdoms of the world. However, Jesus heard the Word of God, believed it, and was obedient to what He heard. God spoke to Jesus through the Word.

God speaks to us through Scripture that the Holy Spirit brings to our mind. Through it, we may be given direction, correction, or encouragement. Sometimes God speaks as we are reading our Bibles. One word or sentence may jump off the page or look like it has been highlighted. You may feel as though you have never seen this passage before. *When was it added?* When you experience this happening, know that it is God's "rhema," the personal word given just for you for this moment in time.

Thoughts

God often speaks to us by putting a thought in our mind. Scripture records the story of a woman who had an issue of blood for twelve years. ". . . she *thought*, 'If I could just touch his clothes, I will be healed.' Immediately her bleeding stopped and she felt in her body that she was freed from her suffering" (Mark 5:28–29, authors' emphasis). God had spoken to her through her thoughts.

It is the Holy Spirit who puts the thoughts of God in our mind for "no one knows the thoughts of God except the Spirit of God" (1 Cor. 2:11). It is the Spirit of God who tells us things that we could have no other way of knowing.

When God speaks through our thoughts, often a thought will suddenly pop into our minds. Sometimes it comes like an impression or a nudge. Someone's name will suddenly come into our mind when we have not been consciously thinking about that person. We may simply assume that it is our own thought. However, when that happens, turn to God and ask if it is a thought put there by the Holy Spirit. If so, then we will want to be obedient, lift that person up in prayer, and/or make contact with him or her.

In praying for healing and wholeness, there are times when God puts a thought into the mind of the one praying. Sometimes that thought conveys that there is a certain way to pray for a particular need. When that thought is spoken and the prayer is given, God's Word accomplishes the purpose for which it was sent.

Visions

Many people hear God speak to them through visions or pictures that they see in their mind or spirit. Jesus said that He was doing only what He saw His heavenly Father doing. When God speaks to a person through a vision, He is showing them what is going to happen.

The prophet Joel prophesied that "young men will see visions" (2:28).

The apostle Peter had a vision of a sheet filled with all kinds of animals, reptiles, and birds:

> *Then a voice said to Peter, "Get up Peter; kill and eat." But Peter said, "No, Lord! I have never eaten food that is unholy or unclean." But the voice said to him again, "God has made these things clean so don't call them 'unholy'!"*
>
> **—Acts 10:13–15 NCV**

Peter later interpreted this vision as God's word for him to preach the gospel to the Gentiles.

When we see a vision of what God desires to have done, God has spoken to us and we can pray with confidence, believing that God will accomplish that which has been revealed to us.

Dreams

Scripture records that on several occasions God spoke to persons through dreams. Just as the young will see visions, likewise the old will dream dreams. "Your old men will dream dreams" (Joel 2:28).

Joseph, one of Jacob's twelve sons, dreamed that he and his brothers were in a field, tying bundles of wheat. In the dream, all the bundles bowed down to Joseph's bundles. When Joseph told this dream to his brothers, they became angry. In their anger and jealousy, they eventually sold Joseph to traders and then told their father that wild beasts had killed him.

Joseph was sold into slavery in Egypt and ultimately became the most powerful man next to Pharaoh. Years later, there was a famine in Israel, and Jacob sent his sons to Egypt for grain. The man before whom they needed to bow down was Joseph. The dream that Joseph had had years earlier while still a young man, became a reality (Gen. 37).

Many centuries later, God spoke to another Joseph through a dream. Joseph and Mary were planning to be married when Joseph discovered that Mary was pregnant. Joseph planned to divorce her quietly, but God spoke to him in a dream.

> *Joseph, descendent of David, don't be afraid to take Mary as your wife, because the baby in her is from the Holy Spirit. She will give birth to a son and you will name him Jesus, because he will save his people from their sins.*
>
> —**Matthew 1:20–21** NCV

Joseph followed God's direction in the dream and became the earthly father figure to the Savior of the world.

Please know that not all dreams are from God. However, if a dream remains very clear in detail the next morning, the next week, and the next month, it is likely that God is endeavoring to speak through that dream to make us aware of something that He desires us to know or do.

We should also ask the Holy Spirit if the dream is from God. The Holy Spirit is the Spirit of truth and will reveal to us the truth regarding the dream.

Bears Witness

God also speaks as the Spirit of God bears witness to our spirit. "The Spirit himself testifies with our spirit . . ." (Rom. 8:16).

For those of us who are perceptive or "feeling" people, God may well speak to us by this manner. We may become aware, even as we enter a room, that someone there is hurting, angry, or grieved. This is the Spirit bearing witness to our spirit. We become aware of the presence of God and/or the presence of evil. As we pray, we may feel peace about the subject. Whatever burden was there lifts and everything feels right.

It is also true that if there is a feeling of heaviness or uneasiness, it may be God's Spirit bearing witness to our spirit and giving us warning that something is not right. God often bears witness to our spirit as the Holy Spirit manifests the gift of discernment in our lives.

Prayer intercessors often "hear" God speaking through bearing witness. We are allowed to feel God's heart or feel the burden of someone else so that we may pray for them according to God's will.

Songs

Sometimes God speaks through psalms, hymns, and spiritual songs. There are several instances in Scripture regarding this. Job remembered that the God he worshiped was a God who spoke through songs. "Where is God my Maker, who gives songs in the night?" (Job 35:10).

After Israel had crossed the Red Sea on dry ground, the Egyptian army was destroyed as the waters of the sea flooded back over them. At that point, a song was given by God to Miriam, the sister of Moses and Aaron. She picked up a tambourine and began to dance and sing: "Sing to the Lord, because he is worthy of great honor; he has thrown the horse and its rider into the sea" (Exod. 15:21 NCV).

In the New Testament, we are instructed to "Speak to one another with psalms, hymns and spiritual songs" (Eph. 5:19).

Through Others

God often speaks through others that which God desires us to hear. This is often called a word or prophetic word: "A man [or woman] finds joy in giving an apt reply—and how good is a timely word!" (Prov. 15:23).

The speaking of a prophetic word is one way in which God may speak through other persons. When a prophetic word is spoken to an individual, it generally confirms what God has already spoken to that person or made them aware of beforehand.

The truth of what another says will also witness to our spirit. As we listen to people share their stories during a prayer session, God may highlight a word or sentence. It is as though someone increases the volume of a radio. We will hear it loud and clear. This is similar to the "rhema," or personal word that we receive in Scripture, except that this is an audible revelation of that which God desires us to hear.

Our Response to God's Voice

Hearing Clearly

Sometimes we hear clearly when God speaks and can respond as we are directed by the Holy Spirit. In those times, our obedience in following God's instruction brings about positive results in our own lives and in the lives of those to whom we minister. At other times, our hearing may not be as good, and for a variety of reasons, we may fail to hear that word God desires us to hear.

Hearing Incompletely

Sometimes we hear God's voice and God's word incompletely. That is, we hear in part. Consequently, there may be a tendency to jump to conclusions, without having heard completely what God has said. Scripture reminds us that we "know in part" (1 Cor. 13:12). We also hear in part. Nevertheless, we should not allow fear or doubt to keep us from acting on that which we have heard, nor should it keep us from seeking further guidance from God.

One must use wisdom in sharing what we think God has said. This is important in order to prevent problems or frightening people by overenthusiastic sharing. We are human and there are times when we simply do not hear completely. In those times, we share what it is we sense that God is saying and pray accordingly. If that which is shared is truth from God, the Holy Spirit will use the word to convict (make us aware of our sinfulness or the truth), or encourage or heal (John 16:8–11).

Do Not Hear

There are times when God speaks to us and we simply do not hear. There are too many distractions, our minds are somewhere else, or other issues are crowding in on us and calling for our attention.

Scripture tells us, "We do not know what we ought to pray, but the Spirit himself intercedes for us . . ." (Rom. 8:26). It does not say, "*When* we do not know what to pray," it clearly states that we do not know *what* to pray.

We can be so involved in our daily living that we do not take time to listen, we do not want to hear what God thinks, or we believe that if we hear God, then we would have to obey (and we don't want to!). It could also be that we are in a wilderness time and God seems to be silent—at least, that is how it appears.

In those times when we do not hear God speaking to us, giving direction on what and how we should pray, we simply pray as we feel led to pray, believing that the Holy Spirit leads us to pray in that manner. Often as we begin to pray, we find that the words and direction do come. As we speak, those words become a step of faith for us. And when we take that step, God fills the void and provides the direction.

There Are Blocks to Hearing God

Just as there are blocks to receiving God's Spirit and other blessings from God, so too are there things that block our ability to hear God's voice. These may include:

- unforgiveness
- rebellion
- feeling unworthy
- fear of hearing
- fear of not hearing
- disobedience the last time we heard

Any of these can block our hearing of God's voice. In those times, we need to pray, as did the psalmist: "Search me, O God, and know my heart; test me and know my anxious thoughts. See if there is any offensive way in me, and lead me in the way everlasting" (Ps. 139:23–24).

Discerning What Is Heard

When we endeavor to hear God and to understand what God is saying to us, we must remember that we are listening in the realm of the Spirit. Therefore, it is important that we learn to evaluate what we hear to make sure we are hearing the voice of God.

These guidelines are helpful as we discern the voice of God:

- *Is what I am hearing in harmony with Scripture?* God will never say anything or ask us to do anything that is not in harmony with Scripture, God's Word.

- *Is this the nature of Jesus?* Would Jesus say or do this? That which is being heard must stand in harmony with the life of Jesus as we have come to know Him through Scripture.

- *Does what I am hearing edify me or edify the body of Christ, the church?* That which comes from God always edifies (builds up and strengthens) the individual believer and the church.

- *Does this witness to my spirit?* When something is of God, the Holy Spirit witnesses the truth of it to our spirit.

God still speaks to us today. Since "Jesus Christ is the same yesterday and today and forever" (Heb. 13:8), He still speaks to us in the present as He has in the past. God may speak through an audible voice, a Scripture, a thought, a vision, a dream, a song, a person, or a witness to my spirit.

God may have other ways through which we may hear His voice. Regardless of how He speaks to us, it is then that we experience God's power move in and through our lives. This often brings healing and wholeness to us and others who have needs of which God has made us aware.

The word of knowledge is especially important when praying for physical healing. We ask, "God how would you have me pray for this person?" The actual physical problem may not be as evident as it appears on the surface. God knows the source!

Do not put your faith in your ability to hear God! Put your faith in God's ability to speak to you!

"Call to me and I will answer you and tell you great and unsearchable things you do not know" (Jer. 33:3).

We have found that material from certain chapters is best incorporated into participants' lives when directly followed by a time of practical application. As a result, we will now move directly into a workshop for learning to hear God's voice rather than a group discussion of the reflection questions used in other chapters.

WORKSHOP ON WORD OF KNOWLEDGE

This is a workshop in which the participants will practice hearing God's voice.

In this Time of Asking God how to Pray

1. Select one person as your prayer partner who is not a relative or close friend. Be seated side by side.

2. First, you will each **pray for yourself**. Ask God how He would have you pray for yourself. For example: "God, how or what do You want me to pray about for myself?" Sit quietly and listen (2–3 minutes).

   God may answer and speak to you in any one of the following ways:

Audible Voice	Scripture	Thought
Vision	Dream	Bearing Witness
	Through Song	

   When you sense God's direction as to how and for what to pray, **pray silently** until the workshop facilitator closes the initial prayer time.

3. Now, decide between you and your prayer partner who is Number One and who is Number Two.

4. Number One **sits silently** in the presence of God while Number Two places a hand on the other's shoulder or back at the base of the neck. Ask if that is all right with the person being prayed for. (Some people are uncomfortable being touched).
   Number Two then asks God, "How do you want me to pray for my brother/sister?"
   LISTEN and pray **SILENTLY** according to how you are led by the Holy Spirit. The other person will not hear a word you are saying. The workshop facilitator will close the prayer time (2–3 minutes).

5. Reverse positions with Number Two sitting in the presence of God and Number One placing a hand on his or her shoulder or back. (Again, request permission first.)
   Number One then asks God, "How do you want me to pray for my brother/sister?" Then listen and pray silently according to the Holy Spirit's leading.

6. The workshop facilitator will close the prayer time (2–3 minutes).

Sharing

1. After the one-on-one prayer time, take opportunity to share some feelings in the total group:

   - How does it feel to have **someone pray for you** knowing they first went to God for direction?

   - How does it feel to **pray for someone** after having first gone to God for direction?

2. The two prayer partners will **share with each other** how they felt God led them to pray for one another.

3. Do you feel that your prayer partner was led by God to pray for a very real area of need in your life?

4. Did God lead your prayer partner to pray for the same issue in your life that God talked with you about in your own personal prayer time?

Personal Sharing

The facilitator will ask if anyone would like to share with the total group how God led his or her prayer partner to pray for that special need in his/her life. **Individuals may share their own stories.** We are not free to share another person's story until and/or unless he or she gives us permission to do so.

VII. HEALING THE HUMAN SPIRIT

Any discussion about the healing of the human spirit should lead us to consider the healing of the separation that exists between fallen humankind and its Creator God. We must consider ways in which God, through Christ, redeems from sin, heals our human spirit, and brings us into wholeness in our relationship with God.

Sin, repentance, forgiveness, receiving Jesus as Savior and Lord, and baptism with the Holy Spirit are connected to the healing of the human spirit that occurs through right relationship with God through Jesus Christ by the power of the Holy Spirit.

SCRIPTURE:

The Spirit of the Lord is on me, because he has anointed me to preach good news to the poor. He has sent me to proclaim freedom for the prisoners and recovery of sight for the blind, to release the oppressed, to proclaim the year of the Lord's favor.

—**Luke 4:18–19**

But now you must rid yourselves of all such things as these: anger, rage, malice, slander, and filthy language from your lips. Do not lie to each other, since you have taken off your old self with its practices and have put on the new self, which is being renewed in knowledge in the image of its Creator. Here there is no Greek or Jew, circumcised or uncircumcised, barbarian, Scythian, slave or free, but Christ is all, and is in all.

Therefore, as God's chosen people, holy and dearly loved, clothe yourselves with compassion, kindness, humility, gentleness and patience. Bear with each other and forgive whatever grievances you may have against one another. Forgive as the Lord forgave you. And over all these virtues put on love, which binds them all together in perfect unity. Let the peace of Christ rule in your hearts, since as members of one body you were called to peace. And be thankful. Let the word of Christ dwell in you richly as you teach and admonish one another with all wisdom, and as you sing psalms, hymns and spiritual songs with gratitude in your hearts to God. And whatever you do, whether in word or deed, do it all in the name of the Lord Jesus, giving thanks to God the Father through him.

—**Colossians 3:8–17**

Additional Scripture Readings: Colossians 2:21–23; 3:1–7

New Testament accounts of Jesus' ministry show that His message and His acts of healing were inextricably bound together.

Jesus came as **Redeemer** to set people free from the powers of darkness, the consequences of their fall, and their sin; to reconcile them to their Creator; and, as Peter said, to transfer us into the Kingdom of Light (1 Pet. 2:9–10, paraphrased).

Jesus came as **Savior** to deliver people from death into life. His very name "Jesus" (Joshua, Yeshua) means "God is salvation," carrying with it the meaning that God is our Savior. Savior also means "healer." God is our healer.

Jesus' name carries with it not only the meaning of His mission, but also the authority with which to carry out that mission. Jesus' disciples healed "in His name," they cast out demons "in His name," they baptized "in His name" with total authority of that name.

It is important to note that Jesus had concern for the whole person: spirit, soul, body, and relationships. One of the opening declarations Jesus made about His own ministry was in the synagogue at Nazareth. In Luke 4, he quotes Isaiah 61:1–2, declaring: "The Spirit of the Lord is on me, because he has anointed me to preach good news to the poor. He has sent me to proclaim freedom for the prisoners and recovery of sight for the blind, to release the oppressed, to proclaim the year of the Lord's favor."

At another time, the Jewish leaders chastized Him for healing on the Sabbath. He said to them: "Now if a child can be circumcised on the Sabbath so that the law of Moses may not be broken, why are you angry with me for healing the whole man on the Sabbath?" (John 7:23).

These episodes demonstrate Jesus' concern for persons and their wholeness. He saw them as whole, unified beings—body, mind, spirit—not body *and* mind *and* spirit. What affected one part affected the whole. What touches the spirit, touches the emotions and body as well; what impacts the emotions has consequences for the spirit and body; what affects the body also has its impact on the emotions and spirit.

In our modern treatment of illness, we often tend to believe that we can treat the body without taking into account the soul and the spirit. Consequently, some people never deal with the deep emotional or spiritual traumas that may be the source of their physical maladies.

On the other hand, if we endeavor to deal with a person's spirit totally apart from their physical or emotional needs, we have a religion with words but no power (James 2:14–17).

To talk about healing the spirit and body without considering the emotional hurts of a person's soul is akin to putting Band-Aids on a cancerous tumor.

Jesus' concern was for the healing of the whole person. He forgave sins—**healing of the spirit.** He released persons from prisons of fear, lust, greed, oppression, and rejection—**healing of the soul** (mind, will, and emotions). He delivered from demonic forces—**deliverance**, which often includes healing of the spirit, soul, and body. He healed the sick—**healing of the body**.

The Diseased Spirit

Jesus healed the diseased (dis-eased) spirit. Most diseases are deficiency diseases. That is, we become ill when some essential ingredient is missing from the elements that work together to produce health and wholeness in our bodies. Physically, we feel sick, we look sick, and we are sick, for all symptoms point to that fact.

The same is true with our emotions and our spirit. When these are not healthy, something is missing. Spiritually and emotionally we feel sick, we look sick, and all the symptoms point to the fact that we are sick.

In both the letters to the Ephesians (2:12) and to the Colossians (1:21), the apostle Paul describes the consequence of this missing element as being alienated, without hope, and without God.

When a person is sick in the spirit, something is deficient in their relationship with God; something is missing. That which is missing is a right relationship with God.

This sickness is brought about by the element of sin present in the human spirit. Sin means basically to miss the mark, to aim at a target and miss it. Sin is that diseased condition of the human spirit that serves to keep us from what God intends us to be in the first place. Sin is that condition that causes spiritual sickness and alienation from God.

Since the fall of Adam and Eve, natural man has suffered in his spirit—alienated from God. To be alienated, without hope, and without God is to be sick in the spirit, critically ill! This disease leads to eternal death.

The human condition, then, is a diseased spirit in which sin has worked to alienate the person from the relationship with God that brings with it spiritual health and wholeness.

Deliverance from personal sin is referred to as the healing of the spirit. It can take place at the time of our initial encounter with God as well as throughout all our faith journey. Sin clings close, but "where sin abounds, God's grace abounds all the more" (Rom. 5:20, paraphrased).

Symptoms of the Spirit's Condition

When a person is physically ill, certain symptoms appear that indicate an unhealthy condition in the body. The same is true when there is an illness in the human spirit. Certain symptoms appear that indicate that the spirit is not whole and that the person is suffering in his or her relationship with the Creator God.

The Eyes

One of the first symptoms of a diseased spirit is the eyes. Jesus said, "The eye is the lamp of the body. If your eyes are good, your whole body will be full of light. But if your eyes are bad, your whole body will be full of darkness. If then the light within you is darkness, how great is that darkness!" (Matt. 6:22–23).

Often the first thing a physician checks relative to physical illness is the eye. Next to the brain, the eye is the most complex organ in the body. In addition to its primary purpose of providing vision, it also reflects the state of our physical being. Sickness within the physical body will often be seen in eyes that are dull and in which there is no light.

The same is true with illness in the human spirit. The physical eyes lack luster and brightness; they are dull, expressionless, hard, and flat in appearance.

There is truly a darkness about them, which is a good indication that something is not right in a person's relationship with God. Considering Matthew 6:23 mentioned above, that statement of Jesus may mean, "If you interpret the darkness within you as light; if you accept error as truth, you are worse off than you thought. You truly have a diseased spirit."

Personal Countenance

Another symptom of a diseased spirit is found in our personal countenance. Simply put, a person with a diseased spirit feels sick, looks sick, and acts sick. They appear to be tired and weary. They have the appearance of a person who is depressed. They seem to lack a sense of direction or purpose for their life. There is often a look of hopelessness in their face. There is no "glow" in their countenance.

The absence or presence of the fruit of the Holy Spirit gives good indication of the level of our spiritual health. When a person is sick in the spirit, there is an absence of joy, peace, patience, kindness, goodness, faithfulness, gentleness, and self-control. These are absent because God's quality of love (agape) is not present in the person's life.

The absence of the fruit of the Spirit is a good indication that we have unhealthy spirits. These fruit are all evidences of the presence of God's Holy Spirit in our lives. Where the Spirit of the Lord is, these spiritual fruit abound. It is impossible to have spiritual health without spiritual fruit.

Attitudes

Negative attitudes such as fear, unforgiveness, and bitterness may lead to bondage to demonic forces and are also symptoms of a diseased spirit. When we allow these attitudes to rob us of a sense of direction and purpose for our lives, we experience illness in our spirits.

Negative attitudes can also result in the loss of hope. Hope means to have absolute confidence and trust. For the Christian, that confidence and trust is in Jesus Christ. When we are without hope, we are without confidence and trust; our spirits are not at ease, they are diseased.

Religiosity

At the other end of the spectrum, symptoms of a diseased spirit may show up as religiosity (being excessively religious), self-righteousness, spiritual pride, bondage to religious legalism, and judgmentalism. Spiritual arrogance indicates that something is wrong in the human spirit and points to a need for healing. Pride serves to alienate us from God, for then self becomes god.

Prescriptions and Therapies for Healing

When a person is physically ill, that illness can usually be treated by a prescription to provide medication to make up for the deficiency in the elements in the human body. As part of the healing process, a person might also need therapy or long-term care in order for the body to regain and retain its vigor.

God has provided treatment for a diseased spirit.

Scripture provides prescriptions and therapies by which the human spirit may be healed. An Old Testament prescription reads:

> *If my people, who are called by my name, will humble themselves and pray and seek my face and turn from their wicked ways, then will I hear from heaven and will forgive their sin and will heal their land.*
>
> **—2 Chronicles 7:14**

Healing of the spirit—healing of that relationship between God and us—involves:

- repentance
- prayer
- confession
- forgiveness
- absolution

We are to humbly acknowledge the sinful condition in which we find ourselves. We identify the sin for what it is. We are not to rationalize sin, pretend it doesn't exist, or try to make excuses for it, but acknowledge it. Then God can heal it.

Our part in the healing of our spirit is to repent and confess the sin condition. God's part is to forgive and to absolve us, setting us free from its hold on our lives.

In giving a New Testament prescription for ongoing therapy, Jesus said:

> *Come to me, all you who are weary and burdened, and I will give you rest. Take my yoke upon you and learn from me, for I am gentle and humble in heart, and you will find rest for your souls. For my yoke is easy and my burden is light.*
>
> —Matthew 11:28–30

Here, Jesus is talking about healing for the soul, which is the seat of our will and our emotions. The same therapy also works for the spirit.

When our spirits are weary and burdened down, we come to Jesus who provides rest. His spirit (heart) is gentle and humble and He can provide us with that same gentle and humble spirit.

Additional therapy for the healing of the spirit is:

The Study of God's Word

> *He sent forth his word and healed them; he rescued them from the grave.*
>
> —Psalm 107:20

> *I am the LORD who heals you.*
>
> —Exodus 15:26

The study of God's Word reminds us of all the promises God makes to those who desire to be in right relationship with their Creator.

Through the Word of God, the Holy Spirit nurtures our spirit.

Worship and Praise

Worship and praise bring healing to our spirits as they fill us with the life-giving presence of God's Holy Spirit. When we sing praise to God, it releases a spiritual medicine that brings healing to the heart. When we worship, our spirit stands in the presence of the God who heals.

The Sacraments

In worship, we participate in and receive the sacraments of Holy Communion and baptism. Through the power of the Holy Spirit, we experience the presence of the Risen Lord in the sacraments, whose presence brings change to our spirit.

We are baptized into the name of our Lord Jesus Christ and so become one with Him and with His body, the church.

When we partake of the bread and wine of Holy Communion, the Eucharist, we not only remember the act of the Last Supper that Jesus shared with His disciples, but we also remember that we also share in His life, death, and resurrection. We are alive in Christ.

When I realize that "[I] died, and [my] life is now hidden with Christ in God" and "When Christ, who is [my] life, appears, then [I] also will appear with him in glory," then I can better understand that I am healed in my spirit (Col. 3:3–4, paraphrased).

This realization is brought about by the work of God's Holy Spirit in my life. It is God's Spirit that draws me to God in the first place. It is also God's Spirit who sanctifies or cleanses my life of all unrighteousness—the things that work to keep me separated from God. God is not only "faithful and just to forgive my sins," but also to "cleanse me from all unrighteousness." (1 John 1:9, paraphrased).

It is the Holy Spirit who enables me to maintain a right relationship with God. It is God's Holy Spirit who empowers me to "walk worthy of the calling with which you [I] were [was] called" (Eph. 4:1 NKJV).

When I am healed in my spirit, by the power of the Holy Spirit and through what Jesus did for me at the cross, I am able to walk in a righteous (right) relationship with God.

A healed spirit carries with it certain evident results.

The Healed Spirit

When persons experience healing in their physical bodies, there is a certain new vigor related to that healing. They feel healthy. They look healthy. They are healthy.

Likewise, when persons experience healing in their spirits, there is a certain new vigor related to that healing. They feel right. They look right. They are right; they are in right relationship with God.

In that right relationship, they no longer experience alienation; they are no longer without hope; no longer without God. They experience inner peace and an assurance of God's love and acceptance.

When persons are healed in their spirits, they experience justification, salvation, deliverance, and atonement, being at one with God.

The initial result of the healing of the spirit is new birth. Persons who are healed in their spirits are born of the Holy Spirit into a new relationship with Jesus Christ. The healing of the spirit opens the door to God's Holy Spirit to work the miracle of healing and wholeness in all other areas of life.

Following new birth, there is new fruit of the Holy Spirit present. Love, joy, and peace enter a person's heart and life. There is a new desire to praise God and to give thanks to God for His mercy and grace.

Healing of the spirit begins the spiritual journey that includes allowing the Holy Spirit to develop the additional spiritual fruit of patience, kindness, goodness, faithfulness, gentleness, and self-control.

Spiritual healing frees people to lean on the Holy Spirit when tempted to sin. In that temptation, they learn that God provides a way of escape, which is through the temptation to victory over it.

> *No temptation has seized you except what is common to man. And God is faithful; he will not let you be tempted beyond what you can bear. But when you are tempted, he will also provide a way out so that you can stand up under it.*
>
> **—1 Corinthians 10:13**

With a healed spirit, there is release from the fear of death, for by Jesus' death He destroyed "him who holds the power of death—that is, the devil—and free[d] those who all their lives were held in slavery by their fear of death" (Heb. 2:14–15).

The healed spirit is at peace with God, in right relationship with God, and trusts in God alone for life abundant on earth and eternal in heaven.

The following is a quote from John Wesley's sermon, "Original Sin." In it, he offers the means whereby persons may recognize and be healed of that which separates them from their Creator God. Though he uses the word "soul," he means more than our psyche, our will, and our emotions. He speaks of the human spirit.

> *We may learn from hence, in the Third place, what is the proper nature of religion, of the religion of Jesus Christ. It is* therapeia psuches, *God's method of healing a soul which is thus diseased. Hereby the great Physician of souls applies medicines to heal this sickness; to restore human nature, totally corrupted in all its faculties. God heals all our Atheism by the knowledge of Himself, and of Jesus Christ whom he hath sent; by giving us faith, a divine evidence and conviction of God, and of the things of God, in particular, of this important truth, "Christ loved me and gave himself for me." By repentance and lowliness of heart, the deadly disease of pride is healed; . . .*
>
> *Ye know that the great end of religion is, to renew our hearts in the image of God, to repair that total loss of righteousness and true holiness which we sustained by the sin of our first parent. Ye know that all religion which does not answer this end, all that stops short of this, the renewal of our soul in the image of God, after the likeness of Him that created it, is no other than a poor farce, and a mere mockery of God, to the destruction of our own soul. . . .*
>
> *Keep to the plain, old faith, "once delivered to the saints," and delivered by the Spirit of God to our hearts. Know your disease! Know your cure! Ye were born in sin: Therefore, "ye must be born again," born of God. . . . In Adam ye all died: in the second Adam, in Christ, ye all are made alive. . . . Now, "go on from faith to faith," until your whole sickness be healed; and all that "mind be in you which was also in Christ Jesus!"*
>
> —**Wesley's Sermons**

As discussed, the process for healing the spirit includes:

- Acknowledge the condition.
- Confess the sin that separates or alienates us from God and from wholeness in the spirit.
- Hear God pronounce absolution that we are clean according to the promise of God's Word.
- Affirm that God forgives and we are to accept that forgiveness, then thank God for the new life that is ours in Christ Jesus.

Receiving Jesus into our heart and life is the most powerful way to experience healing in the spirit.

We have found that material from certain chapters is best incorporated into participants' lives when directly followed by a time of practical application. As a result, we will now move directly into a workshop for healing of the spirit rather than a group discussion of the reflection questions used in other chapters.

WORKSHOP ON HEALING THE SPIRIT

Whether as individuals or in a small group, the following questions help guide our thoughts relative to the healing of our spirits. Please share with others at a level that is comfortable for you.

1. Where are you struggling in your relationship with God?
2. Do you feel alienated, without hope, and without God?
3. Do you believe in God? If you desire to receive Jesus into your life, you may do it now.
4. Have you been baptized with the Holy Spirit?
5. Have you lost your first love for God?
6. Is there fear in your life?
7. Is there unforgiveness in your heart?
8. Do you tend to mix kingdom and world standards in your life?
9. Do you have an inability to love after the example of Jesus?
10. Are you lukewarm or apathetic in your discipleship?
11. Do you feel competent to meet your own needs without God's help?
12. Are you unable to share your faith?
13. Do you desire a more personal relationship with God's Holy Spirit?

Have a time of sharing in small groups (preferably three in each group) and then pray for each other as directed by the Lord.

Prayer

You may wish to pray the following (or similar) prayer to commit or recommit your life to God in Christ.

"Gracious and loving God, thank You for loving me and sending Your Son, Jesus, to die for me. I confess my sins and I name them in my heart. I ask You to forgive me and I thank You for Your forgiveness according to the promise in Your Word.

"Jesus, I invite You to come into my heart. I believe that You died for my sins and that You rose again from the dead and gave me eternal life. I invite You to come into my heart, live in me, and be the Lord of my life.

"Jesus, I ask You to baptize me with Your Holy Spirit. Fill me with Your eternal love and presence so that I may be totally Yours—spirit, mind, and body. Holy Spirit, make me into the image of Jesus so that my life may be like His.

"Thank You, loving God, for Your Son and Your Spirit. Thank You for cleansing me of anything that is not in harmony with Your will for my life. Thank You for filling me with Your love, joy, and peace. Thank You for giving me a new and eternal life. Amen."

VIII. FORGIVENESS AND THE HEALING PROCESS

We're now ready to focus on forgiveness and its importance in the process of our healing and wholeness; as we do, we'll consider what forgiveness is, what it is not, what it does, and what it does not.

The purpose of this is to have a clear:

- theological understanding of forgiveness.

- understanding of the part that forgiveness plays in God's plan for humanity.

- insight to how it is demonstrated in the life of Jesus.

- direction on how we learn to forgive, following Jesus' example.

It is also important to realize the impact that unforgiveness has upon our spiritual, emotional, and physical well-being.

SCRIPTURE:

Therefore, the kingdom of heaven is like a king who wanted to settle accounts with his servants. As he began the settlement, a man who owed him ten thousand talents was brought to him. Since he was not able to pay, the master ordered that he and his wife and his children and all that he had be sold to repay the debt. The servant fell on his knees before him. "Be patient with me," he begged, "and I will pay back everything." The servant's master took pity on him, canceled the debt and let him go. But when that servant went out, he found one of his fellow servants who owed him a hundred denarii. He grabbed him and began to choke him. "Pay back what you owe me!" he demanded. His fellow servant fell to his knees and begged him, "Be patient with me, and I will pay you back." But he refused. Instead, he went off and had the man thrown into prison until he could pay the debt. When the other servants saw what had happened, they were greatly distressed and went and told their master everything that had happened. Then the master called the servant in. "You wicked servant," he said, "I canceled all that debt of yours because you begged me to. Shouldn't you have had mercy on your fellow servant just as I had on you?" In anger his master turned him over to the jailers to be tortured, until he should pay back all he owed. This is how my heavenly Father will treat each of you unless you forgive your brother from your heart.

—Matthew 18:23–35

And do not grieve the Holy Spirit of God, with whom you were sealed for the day of redemption. Get rid of all bitterness, rage and anger, brawling and slander, along with every form of malice. Be kind and compassionate to one another, forgiving each other, just as in Christ God forgave you.

—**Ephesians 4:30–5:1**

Additional Scripture Readings: Matthew 18:15–22; Ephesians 5:2

Forgiveness is a major key to healing and wholeness in spirit, soul, body, and relationships. It is the word used by God to free humanity from its sinful, alienated, and estranged relationship with God. It is the word that sets people free from bondage in which they find themselves because of an offense that has been committed against them, or which they have committed against another.

Then Peter came to him and said, "Lord, how often shall my brother sin against me, and I forgive him? Up to seven times?" Jesus said to him, "I do not say to you, up to seven times, but up to seventy times seven."

—**Matthew 18:21–22** (NKJV)

If you forgive anyone his sins, they are forgiven; if you do not forgive them, they are not forgiven.

—**John 20:23**

Forgiveness is that powerful Word of God that "goes out from [God's] mouth: It will not return to [God] empty, but will accomplish what [God desires] and achieve the purpose for which [God] sent it" (Isa. 55:11).

- ***Upward***: Forgiveness opens the door to reconciliation and restoration of relationships between God and persons.

- ***Outward***: Forgiveness accomplishes the goal of reconciliation between persons who have experienced alienation from each other.

- ***Inward***: Forgiveness brings peace to those who harbor negative and destructive attitudes toward themselves or others. Forgiveness is a major key to healing and wholeness—especially of relationships.

What Forgiveness Is

In legal terms, forgiveness means to "cancel the debt." Forgiveness is the giving up of resentment or the claim to requital on account of a debt (offense) committed by someone else. It is canceling the demands (debt) held against someone else because of an offense, or perceived offense he or she has committed so that love and acceptance may flow once again. Forgiveness is hard, but it is a basic requirement for positive Christian living and relationships.

What Forgiveness Is Not

Just as it is helpful to understand what forgiveness is, so it is also helpful to understand what forgiveness is not. Forgiveness is not:

- pretending that the offense never happened. Denial is not the same as forgiveness.
- saying that the offense did not hurt.
- saying that what happened was all right.
- giving permission for the offense to happen again.
- absolving a person of the responsibility for their act.
- the immediate reestablishment of trust.
- a feeling.
- optional for a Christian. It is a commandment.

Forgiveness Is the Nature of God

Forgiveness has its roots in God. Forgiveness is an act of God's will and the nature of God. It is God's will to forgive and God wills to forgive. God wills to cancel the demands held against us because of our offense (sin) against God, so that love and acceptance may flow between God and us. God is offended by sin, yet God chooses to forgive the offense.

The prophet Jeremiah spoke God's will: "for I will forgive their iniquity, and I will remember their sin no more" (Jer. 31:34 KJV). That same promise is repeated in Hebrews 10:17 as the writer of this letter quotes the prophet. God wills to *forgive* iniquities and God wills to *not remember* them anymore. This is substantiated in the promise that love "keeps no record of wrongs" (1 Cor. 13:5).

God's forgiveness is also unilateral. That is, God initiates forgiveness. Scripture tells us that God's love is shown for us in this, that "while we were still sinners, Christ died for us" (Rom. 5:8).

The nature of God's forgiveness, then, is that God cancels all the demands placed against us by the law because of the offense committed against God by our sin. In order for love to be able to flow again between God and us, God wills to forgive that sin and God wills to not remember it anymore. "As far as the east is from the west, so far has he removed our transgressions from us" (Ps. 103:12).

Forgiveness Demonstrated in the Life of Jesus

God's quality of forgiveness is demonstrated in the life of Jesus. Jesus is forgiveness personified—forgiveness in the flesh. As Jesus forgave persons, He reflected God's forgiving nature.

At one point in His ministry Jesus said, "I only do what I see my Father doing" (John 5:19, paraphrased). Jesus had no question about His own ability or authority to forgive sins, for that ability and authority was given to Him by God.

Forgiveness was a part of Jesus' daily ministry. There is no New Testament story that indicates that any individual ever asked Jesus to forgive him or her. Yet, Jesus initiated forgiveness on several occasions. He did it as an act of His will and He did it unilaterally. He initiated it regardless of the response of the one who was forgiven.

When the paralytic was brought to Jesus for physical healing, Jesus spoke the words of forgiveness. "Son, your sins are forgiven" (Mark 2:5). On another occasion, when a sinful woman anointed Jesus, He said to His host, "I tell you, her many sins have been forgiven" (Luke 7:47).

When Jesus came into contact with Zacchaeus, the hated tax collector, He saw that Zacchaeus was one of God's chosen people and said, "Today salvation has come to this house, because this man, too, is a son of Abraham. For the Son of Man came to seek and to save what was lost" (Luke 19:9–10).

A woman caught in the act of adultery was brought to Jesus by the leaders to see if He would judge this act in keeping with the law, which said she should be put to death. After all the accusers had left because He pointed out their own sins to them, Jesus said to the woman, "Has no one condemned you? . . . Then neither do I condemn you. . . . Go now and leave your life of sin" (John 8:1–11).

While hanging on the cross, Jesus spoke to one of the thieves hanging beside Him, "I tell you the truth, today you will be with me in paradise" (Luke 23:43). The thief had broken the law that says, "You shall not steal" (Exod. 20:15). Jesus forgave him. He canceled the debt.

The crowning act of forgiveness in Jesus' life and ministry came as He hung on the cross, looked down on the crowd of persons who had been instrumental in His crucifixion, and said, "Father, forgive them, for they do not know what they are doing" (Luke 23:34). Jesus interceded for those who crucified Him. Their offense against God was to kill God's own Son. Yet God willed to forgive them, and the proof of that forgiveness is made evident in the Resurrection.

Jesus demonstrated the nature of God's forgiveness. It is God's will to forgive and God forgives unilaterally regardless of the response of the one toward whom it is directed and often before anyone even asks to be forgiven. However, it is important for us to ask, so that we might know and experience forgiveness in our relationship with God.

Jesus Taught Forgiveness

Jesus not only demonstrated forgiveness in His life and ministry, He modeled it for His disciples and taught it to them. When He was teaching His disciples how to pray, at their request, that prayer included, "Forgive us our trespasses (debts) as we forgive those who trespass against us" (Matt. 6:12 and Luke 11:4, paraphrased).

At another time, Peter asked Jesus, "'Lord, how often shall my brother sin against me, and I forgive him? Up to seven times?' Jesus said to him, 'I do not say to you, up to seven times, but up to seventy times seven'" (Matt. 18:21–22 NKJV).

At yet another time He said, "If your brother [or sister] trespasses and repents, forgive—even seven times a day" (Luke 17:3–4, paraphrased). Jesus taught that forgiveness is continuous, focusing not on a minimum or maximum number of times, but upon a lifestyle that reflects God's nature. Forgiveness is to be lived out in human life as it was demonstrated in the life of Jesus, who understood God's quality of forgiveness.

Forgiveness Is a Lifestyle

Forgiveness on the divine and human level is closely tied together. Jesus said, "And whenever you stand praying, forgive, if you have anything against any one; so that your Father . . . may forgive you . . ." (Mark 11:25 RSV), and, "Forgive, and you will be forgiven" (Luke 6:37).

Jesus demonstrated and taught forgiveness. He expected it to be the norm for the lives of those who would be His disciples. Forgiveness is the gospel. It is the good news proclaimed by Jesus, the disciples, and the early church.

Following the resurrection, Jesus appeared to His disciples and said:

> "Peace be with you! As the Father has sent me, I am sending you." And with that he breathed on them and said, "Receive the Holy Spirit. If you forgive anyone his sins, they are forgiven; if you do not forgive them, they are not forgiven."
> —John 20:21–23

On the road to Damascus, Jesus appeared to Saul (Paul), and said:

> Now get up and stand on your feet . . . I am sending you to them to open their [Gentiles] eyes and turn them from darkness to light, and from the power of Satan to God, so that they may receive forgiveness of sins and a place among those who are sanctified by faith in me.
> —Acts 26:16–18

In the early church, wherever the gospel was proclaimed, the message of forgiveness was a part of that gospel: "If we confess our sins, he [God] is faithful and just and will forgive us our sins and purify us from all unrighteousness" (1 John 1:9).

Jesus demonstrated—He role-modeled—God's forgiving nature. He willed to forgive and He forgave unilaterally. Not only did He demonstrate and teach what God's forgiveness is like, He expected that same quality of forgiveness to be foundational in discipleship. Jesus expects that same quality of forgiveness to be lived out in the life of His body, the church, as it reflects the name of Him who is its head, Jesus.

Forgiveness Is a Learned Trait

Forgiveness is not instinctive to the human personality; it is a learned trait. Christians learn forgiveness as we imitate the nature of God as seen in Jesus Christ. We are instructed in God's Word to:

> Get rid of all bitterness, rage and anger, brawling and slander, along with every form of malice. Be kind and compassionate to one another, **forgiving each other, just as in Christ God forgave you. Be imitators of God, therefore, as dearly loved children** and live a life of love, just as Christ loved us and gave himself up for us as a fragrant offering and sacrifice to God.
> —**Ephesians 4:31–5:2, authors' emphasis**

Love is the prototype of all positive attitudes. The disciples of Jesus were to be known by their love: "All men will know that you are my disciples, if you love one another" (John 13:35).

Bitterness is the prototype of all negative attitudes, for out of bitterness grows all the other negative attitudes that impact our lives. Rage and anger are the emotional expressions of the bitterness that is in our hearts. Brawling and slander are the physical and verbal expressions of the bitterness in our hearts. Malice is premeditated evil that finds its source in the bitterness that resides in our hearts.

Bitterness in the heart is one of the major causes of heart disease. It affects the autonomic nervous system which, in turn, affects the arteries, veins, and blood vessels in our bodies. Bitterness—and the negative attitudes that go with it—causes constriction of the circulatory system and ultimately plays a major role in bringing about heart problems. "Get rid of all bitterness," said the apostle Paul. And for good reason!

Instead, we are to practice forgiveness, as we have been forgiven, and live a life of love patterned after the life of Jesus. We are to imitate God as beloved children.

Unforgiveness

Scripture states that the Israelites rebelled and grieved the Holy Spirit of God (Isa. 63:10). Rebellion grieves the Holy Spirit.

Unforgiveness is rebellion; it is a sin. Cancer cells are rebel cells in the body. As cancer works to destroy the human body, so unforgiveness works like cancer in the human spirit. Much sickness is related to unforgiveness. An estimated 80–90 percent of all illnesses are psychosomatic, involving both the psyche (mind/attitudes) and the soma (body). Many forms of arthritis, nerve disorders, headaches, ulcers, colon trouble, stress, and heart disease have been shown to be connected with bitterness, resentment, and the harboring of unforgiveness.

It takes energy to hold on to a grudge. Speaking forgiveness is difficult, but harboring unforgiveness is deadly. Speaking forgiveness is totally different from thinking it or talking about it. It is essential that we speak the words aloud, so they can go out and accomplish their purpose (Isa. 55:11).

We learn through Jesus that forgiveness is an act of our will and that it is unilateral. We initiate forgiveness. Forgiveness is not optional for the Christian. It is a requirement for effective and productive Christian living. Forgiveness plays a key role in the healing of the human spirit; emotional traumas; physical illnesses; and relationships with God, others, and ourselves. Forgiveness is not the healing, but without it, healing never happens.

IDEAS FOR REFLECTION

Please share at a level that is comfortable for you.

1. Discuss what forgiveness is and what it is not.
2. Are you aware of other definitions for forgiveness?
3. How do we know that forgiveness is an act of God's will?
4. What in Scripture indicates that God initiates forgiveness?
5. What is the greatest example of God's forgiveness of humanity's sin?
6. Would you agree with the statement that forgiveness is a learned trait?
7. How important is forgiveness to the healing process?
8. What part do bitterness and unforgiveness play in our illnesses?
9. Do you agree that unforgiveness is rebellion and sin?
10. How do we know that God is a forgiving God?

IX. PRACTICING FORGIVENESS

We may talk about forgiveness, receive more information on forgiveness and meditate on its importance to health and wholeness. At the same time, it is possible to have the information yet fail to apply it to the situations and needs of our lives. We're now going to deal with the practical application of those theological facets of forgiveness.

God's forgiveness demonstrated in the life of Jesus and made possible today through the work of the indwelling Holy Spirit is meant to be used. The purpose is to bring healing, wholeness, reconciliation, and freedom to persons bound by attitudes and actions that could bring disaster in a life.

SCRIPTURE:

I tell you the truth, whatever you bind on earth will be bound in heaven, and whatever you loose on earth will be loosed in heaven. Again, I tell you that if two of you on earth agree about anything you ask for, it will be done for you by my Father in heaven. For where two or three come together in my name, there am I with them.

—Matthew 18:18–20

Additional Scripture Readings: Matthew 18:15–17, 21–35

There are three areas in which we need to practice forgiveness:

- In our relationship with God
- In our relationship with other people
- In our relationship with ourselves

Forgiveness in Our Relationship with God

We know that God works through Jesus Christ to forgive us our sin. We recall that, "If we confess our sins, he [God] is faithful and just and will forgive us our sins and purify us from all unrighteousness" (1 John 1:9). That is the truth! God does in fact forgive sin, and many times, God is more ready and willing to forgive than we are ready and willing to ask or receive.

One way to ask for God's forgiveness is to say a simple prayer like this one: "God, Your Word tells us that if I confess my sin, You are faithful and just to forgive me. Father, I confess my sin [*name the sin*]. I repent of that sin and I ask You to forgive me. Thank You, Lord, for Your forgiveness."

Do you know that God has forgiven you? How do you know? There are two basic ways to know that God has forgiven us. First is believing the promise of God's Word that if we confess, God will forgive. The second is that we feel in our spirits the witness of the Spirit that we are forgiven.

Receiving Forgiveness

Do you accept God's forgiveness? It is one thing to know that God forgives, but it is another thing to receive it. It is helpful to say aloud, "In the name of Jesus Christ, I am forgiven." And if you are ministering with someone else, it is important for him or her to hear you say that, in the name of Jesus Christ, he or she is forgiven.

We know that God's forgiveness is unilateral and that God wills it. God does, in fact, cancel all demands of the Law that are held against us due to our offenses toward God through our sin. We are a forgiven people!

However, what do we do when we harbor feelings against God? What if, in some way, we believe that God has failed us? What if we feel that God has not fulfilled the promises made in His Word nor answered our prayers, especially when we have cried out in despair for so long?

Like the psalmist, we may feel or say:

Will the Lord *reject us forever?*
Will he never show his favor again?
Has his unfailing love vanished forever?
Has his promise failed for all time?
Has God forgotten to be merciful?
Has he in anger withheld his compassion?

—**Psalm 77:7–9**

What do we do with those feelings? Do we express them? One way of dealing with hurt, though not a positive one, is to suppress it. However, when we suppress any negative feelings that we may harbor against God, we are not dealing with the truth. It is in knowing and dealing with the truth that we are set free, and Satan loses a foothold in our lives.

However, if persons feel under condemnation from God, it is difficult to help them in other areas of healing. The whole healing process involves the ability to see Jesus as a Friend who desires to set us free from any bondage that we may experience.

God does not need our forgiveness, for who is the infinite, immortal, all-wise God that He should be forgiven by finite mortals? God spoke through the prophet Isaiah:

You turn things upside down, as if the potter were thought to be like the clay! Shall what is formed say to him who formed it, "He did not make me"? Can the pot say of the potter, "He knows nothing"?

—Isaiah 29:16

It is we who need to deal with our feelings toward God, and when we perceive that God has failed to fulfill a promise or answer a prayer, we need to acknowledge it. We need to recognize toward whom our anger or frustration is directed and tell God. Confession and repentance must follow.

At times like that, we might say, "God, I feel that You have forsaken me and have not answered my prayer. I confess my sin of unbelief and lack of trust in You. I have not believed the promise of Your Word that You would not forsake me. Please forgive me for my wrong attitude toward You. Thank You for Your forgiveness. Amen."

Forgiveness in Our Relationships with Other People

The practical application of forgiveness takes place as we work it out in our relationships with other people.

> Then Peter came to Him and said, "Lord, how often shall my brother sin against me, and I forgive him? Up to seven times?" Jesus said to him, "I do not say to you, up to seven times, but up to seventy times seven."
>
> —Matthew 18:21–22 (NKJV)

This is not a literal four hundred ninety times, though that would certainly be a good start, but it means that forgiveness is embedded in our very lives and is continuously involved in all our relationships.

"And whenever you stand praying, forgive, if you have anything against any one; so that your Father . . . may forgive . . ." (Mark 11:25 RSV). It is not possible to live in this world without receiving hurts from others. Regardless of the hurt, trauma, or rejection, it is essential that we forgive; otherwise, we will not be able to receive the forgiveness that God offers us. An unforgiving heart does not have the ability to receive forgiveness.

It is not enough to think forgiveness; it must be spoken aloud so that it will register in our conscious as well as our subconscious thinking. Sometimes the reluctance to speak forgiveness is not so much the inability to do so, but the willful choice not to forgive. Just as forgiveness is an act of the will, so unforgiveness is also an act of the will.

Though forgiveness of others is critical to emotional health and wholeness, it is not always easy and it often takes time.

Forgiveness functions somewhat as major surgery. It is the cutting into the old wounds and tumors of bitterness or hurt that infect our lives. That surgical process can be very painful as memories of past offenses are brought to the surface. Forgiveness is not the healing, but it allows the healing process to begin. It deals with an offense in a very positive way. There is still much tenderness in the hurtful area, but the Holy Spirit has been released to accomplish the healing over a period of time.

Forgiveness is the surgery that allows healing to happen!

This sample prayer can help you speak forgiveness and ask for it. "[*Name the offender*], I forgive you for [*name the offenses*]. God, I ask You to forgive me for my attitude [*name your attitude: bitterness, resentment, hatred, etc.*] that I have against [*name*]. Deliver me from the consequences of that attitude. Thank You for Your forgiveness. Amen."

The other person's offense against us is his or her sin. Our attitude toward the offense can be our sin, for which we must seek forgiveness. My attitude toward a person who has offended me has five times the effect of the offense itself. That attitude is what is blocking a right and good relationship with God as well as with the other person.

Seeking forgiveness from others

In addition to speaking forgiveness to those who have offended us, we need also to seek forgiveness from those whom we have wronged. Sometimes we are the offender. We are not always the victim of another's offense; sometimes he or she is a victim of ours. It is we who have spoken the word or committed the act that hurt another person. It is we who have rejected or ignored or maligned them.

As the Holy Spirit brings that to our remembrance, it is important that we take the initial step to seek forgiveness from the person. Jesus said, "If, when you are bringing your gift to the altar you remember that someone has something against you, leave your gift at the altar, go and be reconciled with your brother [or sister], then come and offer your gift" (Matt. 5:23, paraphrased).

Forgiveness in Our Relationship with Ourselves

Many persons are held in emotional prisons by self-condemnation, self-hatred, and self-flagellation. They do not understand the scriptural admonition that there is "therefore now no condemnation for those who are in Christ Jesus. For the law of the Spirit of life in Christ Jesus has set me free from the law of sin and death" (Rom. 8:1–2 RSV).

Often, people can't self-love because of past traumas, overt acts committed by them or against them, ridicule, rejection, etc. Persons reject themselves because of looks, weight, failures, or wrong understanding of their sexuality. They believe their sin is too great, their failure too complete, their rejection too total, to realize any hope of redemption. From their perspective, they are alienated, without hope, and without God.

Maybe they have deserted their families, criticized unjustly, molested children, committed adultery; they may have prostituted their convictions, their minds, and their bodies. They may have participated in immoral and unethical acts, coveted another person's possessions, abandoned their children, and on and on. Self-condemnation has them in prisons whose bars are stronger than steel—and Satan has control.

It is often extremely difficult to forgive ourselves, yet there is a desire and a need within each one of us to do just that. Scripture is just as true for the individual as for the corporate body: "If you forgive the sins of any, they are forgiven; if you retain the sins of any, they are retained" (John 20:23 RSV). If we hold on to the sins that we have committed against our own person, "they are retained," and will be so until we are willing to let the Holy Spirit move us to forgive ourselves.

Would you like to free yourself? Here's a sample prayer: [*Your name*], I forgive you for [*being a failure, for always saying the wrong things, for your insensitivity, for your manipulation of other people, and anything else that you hold against yourself*]. God, please forgive me for my destructive and negative attitude [*name it*] that I hold against myself. I know it is an offense against You for You loved me enough to die for me even while I was still in my sin. Thank You for Your forgiveness. Amen."

So then, what about guilt? We may truly be guilty of the very things that we harbor against ourselves. We do not pretend that it did not happen or that it did not hurt, nor do we believe that God is giving us permission to do it again. However, through forgiveness, God pronounces us "not guilty." Satan will accuse, but God forgives and sets us free from the self-condemnation that has kept us in bondage.

Life is full of hurts and traumas that affect us in negative ways and have an impact upon our personal lives and our relationships with others around us. Unforgiveness keeps us in bondage and in emotional prisons and causes illness in spirit, mind, and body.

Forgiveness, on the other hand, is a key that unlocks prison doors and sets us free from that bondage. Forgiveness is not part of our human nature. It is not instinctive and it is not easy. However, it can be learned, and we learn forgiveness as we imitate the nature of God as revealed in Jesus Christ.

Then, by an act of our will and with the help of the Holy Spirit, we can speak forgiveness and seek forgiveness that heals relationships with God, with others, and with ourselves.

Forgiveness also opens the door to the healing of our spirits, our minds, and our bodies as God's Spirit works to help us be what God had in mind for us to be in the first place—whole persons, filled with God's Spirit and at one with God, with others, and with ourselves.

Forgiveness is canceling the debt. It is canceling any demands that are held against other persons because of offenses they have committed against us.

Forgiveness is not saying that the offense never happened, nor that it didn't hurt. Forgiveness is not saying that the offense was okay, nor is it giving permission for it to happen again. It is not easy and, for the Christian, it is not optional.

Forgiveness is the way that God has provided to bring healing and restoration in spirit, soul, body, and relationships. It is God's powerful Word that goes forth and accomplishes the purpose for which God designed it—reconciliation and restoration.

IDEAS FOR REFLECTION

Please share at a level that is comfortable for you.

Discuss the importance of forgiveness relative to our relationship with God, with others, and with ourselves. Encourage individuals to share personal experiences, as it is comfortable, to illustrate the importance of forgiveness and its relationship to healing and wholeness.

The following discussion questions are designed to help us consider our own need, or to speak or seek forgiveness. It is suggested that time be allotted for ministry and the opportunity to experience forgiveness so that persons may move toward healing and wholeness in their individual lives.

Questions Related to Our Need for Forgiveness

1. Is there anyone who has hurt me?
2. Is there anyone who has hurt me and I have not yet forgiven them?
3. Is there anyone toward whom I hold a grudge?

4. Is there anyone toward whom I have resentment?

5. Is there anyone I hate?

6. Is there anyone with whom I would like to get even?

7. Is there anyone toward whom I harbor ill-will?

8. Is there anyone from whom I need to seek forgiveness for a wrong I have done?

9. Do I need to be reconciled with anyone?

10. Do I really want to do something about it?

Let these questions guide us in our prayer time as we seek the direction of the Holy Spirit to set us free from any attitudes of unforgiveness that may keep us from receiving the freedom which God has for us.

We now move into the workshop to practice forgiveness.

WORKSHOP TO PRACTICE FORGIVENESS

If we confess our sins, he [God] is faithful and just and will forgive us our sins and purify us from all unrighteousness.

—1 John 1:9

In order to practice forgiveness, it is important to get into groups of three and share areas of need for forgiveness. It can be done by following this simple but powerful process.

1. "[*Name the offender*], I forgive you for [*name the offense*]."

2. "God, I ask You to forgive me for my negative attitude [*name the attitude*] toward [*name the offender*]."

3. "God, I thank You for Your forgiveness."

X. HEALING OF EMOTIONAL HURTS

Everyone has life experiences that affect the quality of life in negative ways and require healing in order for life to become positive and productive. This chapter includes ways in which a person may recognize the need for the healing of emotional wounds and traumas that have impacted his or her life.

The healing of our emotional hurts is one way by which the healing Spirit of God can reach into our lives and turn those hurts into positive attributes, developing perseverance, character, and hope.

SCRIPTURE:

He heals the brokenhearted and binds up their wounds.
—Psalm 147:3

Do not conform any longer to the pattern of this world, but be transformed by the renewing of your mind. Then you will be able to test and approve what God's will is—his good, pleasing and perfect will.
—Romans 12:2

For he himself is our peace, who has made the two one and has destroyed the barrier, the dividing wall of hostility.
—Ephesians 2:14

Brothers, I do not consider myself yet to have taken hold of it. But one thing I do: Forgetting what is behind and straining toward what is ahead, I press on toward the goal to win the prize for which God has called me heavenward in Christ Jesus.
—Philippians 3:13–14

If you were asked to recall a special event in your life, what would it be? Would it be a family gathering, a wedding, the birth of a baby, summer camp, or an experience with Jesus?

What are the emotions related to that event? Joy? Excitement? Love?

Now recall a traumatic event in your life. Would it be an accident, a divorce, the death of a loved one, surgery, or rejection by a friend?

What are the feelings that accompany the thoughts of the event? Fear? Horror? Grief?

These emotions are related to our memories. Memories are a mix of good and bad, beautiful and terrible, treasured things and abhored things. We may remember these vividly or submerge them into our subconscious. Either way, these memories have impact and cause us to respond positively or negatively to other life situations.

We live in a fallen world where trauma, pain, sin, embarrassment, rejection, fear, accidents, and death are our constant companions. According to John 10:10, the thief [Satan] is still trying to "steal and kill and destroy." There is no way we can travel through this life without consciously or unconsciously giving and receiving hurts.

The Human Brain

God created us with a brain that records every act, sight, smell, sound, and experience that has ever happened to us. It also records how we interpreted the event—what it said to us, how we responded to it at the time, and what our actions were. These are our memories.

Memories are not simply brain-stored pictures, but they are accompanied by all the feelings, perceptions, thought patterns, attitudes, and tendencies that go with the picture.

For example, the smell of medicine, fresh bread, or old cigarette smoke may bring back a memory of an event that happened to you that included that aroma. The sound of screaming, laughter, or a special song may trigger a memory from your past. The sight of a coffin, an angry spouse, or a field of flowers may push a button of recall to a former time. The feel of coarse material, satin sheets, or rough bark may recall a reaction of pain or pleasure. The taste of alcohol, blood, or banana cream pie may cause a flashback.

Memories include everything that created that total experience. Any one of the five senses may trigger a response in us, either negative or positive, that will cause us to react in the same manner today as we did then.

The event may be distorted because our recall of it may be colored by the intensity of our emotional response at the time. Our conscious mind may have forgotten or buried the incident, but the subconscious does not forget. Past childhood trauma can be as real today as it was when it first happened. As a result, we will most likely respond to a similar incident now even as we did at first.

These are our memories. We never forget anything we have experienced. We may not be able to recall everything at will, but the experience has been catalogued, filed, and stored away in our brain for posterity, and will cause us to react in a variety of ways, most of which are not in the manner God has directed.

Many of these memories may be the result of illness, injury, or someone else's wrong choices. We may well be an innocent party that suffers from something that has happened to us. But whether the trauma is from our wrong choices or no choice at all, our emotions are still affected. Many of these memories cause intense pain in our lives—emotionally, physically, spiritually, and relationally.

The real tragedy is not simply the pain. It is that, because of it, we learn wrong ways of coping with life situations and wrong ways of relating to people until these become our way of life.

The prophet Jeremiah stated, "You can't heal a wound by saying it's not there!" (Jer. 6:14 TLB). That is a very true statement, especially when related to emotional healing.

Ways Trauma Surfaces

If we continue to push down hurts, traumas, and sins, they will surface through one or more of three ways:

- dreams
- erratic behavior, and/or
- physical illness or psychosomatic pain.

Dreams

Not all dreams are from God. However, if we experience a recurring dream with the same theme and its memory lingers for long periods of time, it is most likely the Spirit of God endeavoring to reveal something which needs our care.

Erratic behavior

Sometimes our response to a situation is not in keeping with that situation. We overreact to a very minor stimulus. For example, the elevator door closes and panic starts, or someone touches us and terror begins, or an aroma floats by and loneliness overwhelms us. This may indicate that a similar situation in the past affected us in a profound way, thus creating behavior disproportionate to the present act.

Physical illness or psychosomatic pain

If we continue to push down traumas, they will surface as illness. A Christian psychiatrist friend of ours stated that 80–90 percent of all illness is psychosomatic, meaning that it involves both the mind (psyche) and the body (soma). Emotional illness includes unconscious attitudes as well as conscious emotional states. We use an estimated 50 percent of mental and emotional energy to repress painful memories.

Has a painful event from the past come to mind, and much to your surprise, you find yourself acting as if it had just happened the day before? The reason is that, biochemically, the brain doesn't distinguish whether a memory is short-term or long-term. In other words, the body doesn't know if the event is currently happening or happened years ago. Just thinking about an emotional hurt can cause the body to respond as if those hurts are occurring in that moment. Once the memory is released into biochemical code, the body responds to the chemicals.

The longer we dwell upon old hurts and wounds, the more we build that mental habit into our minds. And the more we allow those emotions to run rampant, the more the body suffers the pain of:

- being fired
- losing a promotion
- feeling the rejection of divorce
- being raped
- losing a loved one
- being ignored again and again and again.

Because of this, it is not uncommon for a person to develop a disease months or years after a severe life crisis. Certain emotions release hormones into the body that can trigger the development of a host of diseases—emotionally and physically.

God did not intend that our emotions trap, torture, or defeat us.

Emotions are given to us so that we may have abundant life. Joy, laughter, sorrow, tears, excitement, love, hope, disappointment, gain, and loss—all these are a part of our emotional makeup.

If we have experienced traumas that caused fear, embarrassment, guilt, rejection, shame, and anxiety, making us unable to function effectively, then there is a need for healing.

Healing Can Happen

God has provided ways for healing to happen, including the healing of memories. One process by which the healing of emotions and memories may occur is to pray for the presence and power of the Holy Spirit to help.

- **Recall the event and relive it again.**
  Bring to the forefront of your thinking the trauma that is indelibly imprinted in the mind.

- **Forgive the person or persons responsible.**
  Forgiveness is vital to the healing of your emotions. Simply say, "[Name], I forgive you for [name the offense]."

- **Ask forgiveness from God for your negative attitude toward that person.**
  You have just forgiven the person who sinned against you, now you must deal with your sin. Your sin is your response to their act. Therefore you say, "God, forgive me for my attitude [name the bitterness] toward [name the person]."

- **Ask the Holy Spirit to give a vision of Jesus being in that scene.**
  Ask Jesus to allow you to see what He would do to heal that situation. His presence brings healing. He will not remove the memory, for that is part of your history, but you will never recall that event again without seeing His presence with you in it.

Healing of emotional hurts enables us to be free of the ongoing emotional struggles that are related to traumas that have happened to us in our past. It is painful to recall those events, but no more painful than that which we experience as we allow them to continue affecting our lives in negative ways.

Forgiving those responsible for the hurt is a difficult thing, but no more difficult than using the energy to suppress the memory. Dealing with resentment and bitterness on a continual basis has a negative impact on our lives and on our relationship with God.

Jesus is the Healer. He is able to make Himself known in every situation and, by the power of His Holy Spirit, transform the hurtful and painful events of our lives into areas of strength in our character and maturity in our faith.

IDEAS FOR REFLECTION

Please share at a level that is comfortable for you.

1. What are some of your good memories and what were the feelings that accompanied them?
2. What are some of your bad memories and what were the feelings that accompanied them?
3. How do you interpret your recurring dreams? Is God speaking to you?
4. When have you experienced erratic behavior in your own life and regarding what situation?
5. Have you experienced any physical maladies as a result of stuffing your feelings?
6. Do any of the questions previously asked in this lesson help in recognizing any need for emotional healing in your own life?

As we move into the workshop on emotional healing, there will be an opportunity to have prayer and experience healing from some of life's traumas.

WORKSHOP ON EMOTIONAL HEALING

After instruction from the facilitator, those in attendance will gather into groups of three. It is suggested that men be with men and women with women during this workshop.

1. Each person will have opportunity to receive ministry and also to pray with the other two people in the group. You are encouraged to share at a level that is comfortable for you.
2. It is important to learn how to determine if there is a need for emotional healing. The questions below may be helpful in that determination.
3. When asking these questions of yourself, it is important to wait before the Lord and allow the Holy Spirit to reveal areas in your life that need God's healing touch before moving forward in the exercise.

Personal Questions to Consider

- What was/is my relationship with my mother and/or father? Was it a good, loving, and trusting relationship or did it involve fear, abuse, desertion, or incest?

- Did I experience rejection as a child? Have there been traumatic experiences resulting in irrational fears? Do I suffer from bouts with depression, worry, or restlessness?

- Do I have memories of past hurts for which I am not able to forgive?

- Do I have recurring and disturbing dreams?

- Do I have a sin that seems to control me?

- Is my life plagued with anger, lust, greed, prejudice, drugs, alcohol, or lack of self-control?

- How do I see myself? Do I feel that I am inferior, a failure, lonely, competitive, unable to relate to others? Do I dislike myself?

- Is there a problem with my sexuality? Do I dislike my own sex or the opposite sex? Do I have same gender sexual attraction? Am I having a problem with masturbation or fantasies? Am I experiencing frigidity and so am unable to respond sexually to my spouse? Am I being sexually promiscuous?

- Is my behavior erratic, responding violently to minor stimuli?

- Am I unable to function positively in some area of my life and relationships?

- Do I have physical illness with psychosomatic pain, fatigue, mental exhaustion, or no medical remedy?

- How is my relationship with God? Do I have close communion with God or do I not relate to Him? Do I feel unworthy and can't do enough to be loved?

- How is my Christian walk? Do I feel unplugged and experience no joy and no victory? Do I have poor spiritual discipline? Do I have rotten spots in the fruit of the Spirit in my life?

The Holy Spirit will bring to mind areas that block our spiritual growth and that keep us from being the people God desires us to be. As we confess the need, the Holy Spirit is free to bring the healing.

The following is a process that may be used, allowing about fifteen minutes per person. Team members will facilitate the process by listening and praying silently as one member works through the process. Touching is not necessary for the process to be effective.

Step 1. Recall the event, the time at which the trauma occurred. Briefly describe it to your fellow team members as to where you were and what happened.

Step 2. Forgive the person or persons you feel were responsible for the hurt. Example: "[*Name*], I forgive you for [*hurt*]."

Step 3. Seek God's forgiveness for your attitude toward that person. Example: "God, forgive me for my attitude [*name it*] toward [*name*]."

Step 4. Ask the Holy Spirit to give you a vision of Jesus' presence in the situation that brought about the trauma. Allow yourself time for this to happen and then describe to the others what Jesus is doing that helps you experience healing of the trauma.

When each member of the team has had opportunity to finish the suggested process, spend the rest of the time praying for other needs of the group and/or sharing how God has touched your life during this special ministry time.

XI. THE GIFT OF DISCERNMENT

The spiritual gift of discernment plays an important part in the healing process. Jesus preached the kingdom of God, forgave sins, healed the sick, and delivered people from bondage to Satan and the kingdom of darkness.

Jesus discerned—saw and interpreted spiritually—the needs of those who came to Him and ministered to them according to that which He discerned. A paralytic was brought to Him by four friends. The man had a need for physical healing, but Jesus discerned that he had a deeper need, that of forgiveness. When He ministered to that deeper need, it also released the man from bondage to that which had paralyzed him (Mark 2:3–12).

The gift of discernment plays a major role in the ministry of healing and wholeness. It functions to help us know if a spirit is of God, Satan, or human origin.

SCRIPTURE:

Dear friends, do not believe every spirit, but test the spirits to see whether they are from God, because many false prophets have gone out into the world.

—1 John 4:1

Discernment is the ability to distinguish between truth and error, right and wrong, reality and unreality.

Different levels of discernment enable persons to live a balanced life by determining that which contributes or is detrimental to that life. The ability to discern right from wrong enables healthy personal and social relationships that contribute to healthy and whole lives.

There are three levels of discernment:

- natural discernment
- spiritual discernment
- spiritual gift of discerning of spirits (1 Cor. 12:10, NKJV)

Natural Discernment

All people have natural discernment to some extent. Natural discernment comes from cultural standards, our system of values, and how we are raised.

It must be acknowledged that natural discernment varies from culture to culture and generation to generation, depending upon the standards, values, and mores of that culture or generation.

That which is discerned as good in one culture may not have the same value attached to it in another culture. That which is discerned as moral in one culture may be considered immoral in another. For example: polygamy may be acceptable and considered a spiritual matter in one culture or religion but seen as immoral and unspiritual in another.

Therefore, natural discernment has limitations and is not dependable when it comes to discerning matters related to spiritual issues since spiritual values vary from culture to culture.

Spiritual Discernment

Spiritual discernment comes as we allow our minds to be renewed in the image of Christ. As our minds are transformed and renewed by the mind of Christ, the world's standards are gradually replaced by the standards of God's kingdom.

We are instructed to "Test all things; hold fast what is good. Abstain from every form of evil" (1 Thess. 5:21–22 NKJV). Spiritual discernment is developed as the Holy Spirit teaches us what is in harmony with Scripture and also with the nature of God.

When discerning whether something is of God, Satan, or human, it is important to ask the following questions: Does this agree with the Word of God? Is it the nature of God as revealed in Jesus? Would Jesus say or do that? Does it edify the church or me? Does my spirit witness to it as truth?

Spiritual discernment develops as we study the Word of God so that we may know the nature of God: "But the fruit of the Spirit is love, joy, peace, patience, kindness, goodness, faithfulness, gentleness and self-control" (Gal. 5:22–23).

As we assimilate the fruit of the Spirit into our thinking, it then becomes evident when the fruit of an unholy or false spirit appears: "But solid food is for the mature, who by constant use have trained themselves to distinguish good from evil" (Heb. 5:14).

The Gift of Discerning Spirits

The gift of discerning of spirits is a supernatural revelation from God. It is a God-given ability to discern, in an instant, if a teaching, prophetic word, person's motivation, spirit, act, etc., finds its origin in God, Satan, or humans.

This gift is given to guard against false teaching and confusion so that people will not be led astray. It is also given to discern good. It will give approval to preaching and teaching that bring forth fresh truth from God. This gift helps the truth of the Lord to be easily discerned.

In Acts 16:16–18, the story is told of a slave girl following Paul and Silas, proclaiming they were men of God: "These men are servants of the most high God, who are telling you the way to be saved." Her words were true. However, they were spoken with false motive, for the wrong purpose, and by the wrong spirit. Paul became upset and cast out a spirit of divination, setting the girl free from bondage to the demonic. Paul used the spiritual gift of discernment.

If God chooses to manifest this gift through a person, that person usually experiences an inner knowing, stirring in the spirit, chill, or hair-tingling sensation indicating that something is either right or wrong.

The person might also have an inner feeling of peace, joy, or love—making them aware of the presence of God in that situation. Or, they may have a feeling of uneasiness, usually indicating that something is not right.

Scripture reminds us that the Holy Spirit bears witness to our spirit (John 15:26, 16:13–14; Rom. 8:16; Heb. 10:15; 1 John 5:6). As the Holy Spirit bears witness to our spirit, we are able to discern that which is or is not of God.

The gift of discernment cannot be learned, but we do need to grow in recognizing it and in being able to use it for God's glory and to set people free from bondage.

For example, while seated beside a woman who was new at a Bible study, one of the members of the group began to sense a heaviness and anger swirling around her. Feeling that it was a poor attitude on her part, she silently chastised herself and totally dismissed it. Later, after prayer, she realized it was an attitude, or spirit, in the woman that was not of God and it was reacting to the Holy Spirit in the lives of the other women in the room. She then knew how to intercede in prayer for the woman to experience freedom in her life.

The only spirit that is from God is the Holy Spirit. The presence of the Holy Spirit is recognized by the evidence of love, joy, and peace, even in the midst of what may be a time of conflicting ideas, words, or actions.

The presence of a wrong or unholy spirit is recognized by situations of turmoil, uneasiness, and factious and angry attitudes. When these situations or attitudes are present, it is easy to discern that they are not from God. Then, one must discern if the source is either human or Satan.

It is important to pray for the spiritual gift of discernment to be manifested in order to make that distinction, so that ministry to the person in need may be effective and productive.

If the situation is caused by human attitude, then a ministry of confession, forgiveness, reconciliation, and healing is necessary. If the situation is caused by an unclean spirit, deliverance prayer is necessary.

The gift of discernment is a top priority in the ministry of deliverance. Deliverance comes from the same root word as "salvation"—to be "called out of the kingdom of darkness into the kingdom of light" (1 Pet. 2:9, paraphrased).

The root word for salvation and deliverance, *soteria*, means to be set free from whatever bondage Satan has us under, whether that is spiritual, emotional, or physical. The gift of discernment enables a person engaged in a ministry of healing and wholeness to know whether an individual's illness or problem is:

- related to emotional difficulties caused by life's traumas,
- a chemical imbalance in the body, or
- the presence of demonic activity in his or her life.

The apostle John said, "Dear friends, do not believe every spirit, but test the spirits to see whether they are from God . . ." (1 John 4:1).

The apostle Paul listed among the spiritual gifts that of distinguishing between spirits (1 Cor. 12:10).

The gift of discerning of spirits or distinguishing between spirits is absolutely essential if persons are to be set free from bondage to that which would seek to destroy their lives.

The gift of discernment is that gift *from* God that enables those in ministry to determine if something is *of* God. When it is of God, the response is praise and thanksgiving. When it is not of God, but of human origin, the response is confession, forgiveness, and reconciliation. When it is of Satan, the response is deliverance from the evil one. Through the use of this gift, people are edified and God's name is glorified.

IDEAS FOR REFLECTION

Please share at a level that is comfortable for you.

1. Do you agree with the statement that natural discernment is a God-given grace for everyone?

2. What are examples from your own life on how you used natural discernment? For example:

    a. How have you discerned what is right or wrong for your children?

    b. How did you discern the qualifications of the candidate for whom you voted in the last school board election?

3. What are some of the questions to ask to help determine if something is of God or not?

4. What do you think it means to "have the mind of Christ"?

5. What are some of the signs of the presence of the Holy Spirit of God?

6. What are some of the signs of the presence of an evil or unholy spirit?

7. What happens when the spiritual gift of discernment is manifested?

XII. THE MINISTRY OF DELIVERANCE

This section presents material related to the presence of demonic or unclean spirits that oppress, harass, or inhabit people's lives. It explains ways in which these spirits may be recognized and how they may be removed.

Jesus had a ministry of deliverance. He delivered people from an alienated relationship into a right relationship with God. He delivered people from sickness to health; from darkness to light; from ignorance to understanding; from spiritual, emotional, and physical bondage to freedom; from death to life. About one-fourth of Jesus' ministry involved delivering persons from demonic or unclean spirits.

SCRIPTURE:

For he will deliver the needy who cry out, the afflicted who have no one to help.
—**Psalm 72:12**

And these signs will accompany those who believe: In my name they will drive out demons; . . .
—**Mark 16:17**

What is deliverance? Deliverance is to be set free from whatever bondage we may be under, whether that bondage is spiritual, emotional, relational, or physical.

The *New Compact Bible Dictionary* by Zondervan Books states that the word deliverance comes from the same root idea as salvation and healing: "To deliver from some danger or evil." Deliverance is to be called "out of darkness into his wonderful light" (1 Pet. 2:9).

Salvation comes as we are brought from an alienated relationship into a right relationship with God. We have been delivered from darkness to light. However, our deliverance does not stop with conversion. It continues on to regeneration, justification, and sanctification. As we walk with the Lord, our lives are continually being delivered as we are enlightened in areas where we have previously been in the dark.

Truly, Jesus is our Deliverer and our Savior from anything that would separate or block us from communication or relationship with God.

Satan, on the other hand, seeks to block communication with God and separate us from God. According to Scripture, Satan:

- has knowledge (Luke 4:10—he knows Scripture);

- has a will (Luke 4:6);

- has the power of death (Heb. 2:14);
- can test humans (Luke 22:31); and
- can send demons or unclean spirits to enter and control people (Acts 16:16–18).

Basically, Satan has two principal powers:

- To accuse. He is the "accuser of our brethren" (Rev. 12:10 NKJV).
- To deceive. He masquerades. "Satan himself masquerades as an angel of light" (2 Cor. 11:14).

Jesus taught the reality of Satan and the presence of demonic, unclean spirits. Today, the gift of discernment reveals the presence of the demonic, unclean spirits and the reality of Satan.

Jesus said of Satan: ". . . he is a liar and the father of lies" (John 8:44), and, "The thief [Satan] comes only to steal and kill and destroy" (John 10:10).

Satan is referred to as the prince of this world and the god of this age: "Now is the time for judgment on this world; now the prince of this world will be driven out" (John 12:31).

Jesus told Peter, "Simon, Simon, behold, Satan has demanded permission to sift you like wheat" (Luke 22:31, NASB).

Peter himself said, "Your enemy the devil prowls around like a roaring lion looking for someone to devour" (1 Pet. 5:8).

James instructs, "Submit . . . to God. Resist the devil . . ." (James 4:7).

The apostle John stated, "The Son of God appeared for this purpose, that He might destroy the works of the devil" (1 John 3:8 paraphrased).

If we believe the Scriptures as truth, then there is a devil whose name is Satan. The ones who do his bidding are demons or unclean spirits. Scripture tells us that demons are fallen angels. When Lucifer (Satan, the devil) was cast down from heaven to earth, one-third of the angels were cast down with him (Isa. 14:12–15; Luke 10:18).

Some say the concept of demons is superstition stemming from the culture of Jesus' time, but if that were so, He who is the Truth would have told the people the truth. Jesus would not have deceived them—and us—into believing in fantasy, a myth, or worse, a lie.

Jesus said on one occasion, "When an unclean spirit goes out of a man . . ." (Matt. 12:43 NKJV). This statement establishes as fact that, to begin with, there was an unclean spirit in the man.

Demons and unclean spirits were present then as well as now, and their work is to keep people in darkness and ignorance of a loving and caring God. Unclean spirits harass and seek to destroy the works of God.

Symptoms of Demonic Activity

Symptoms of demonic activity are often the same as symptoms of psychological sickness. In some cases, the person may be suffering from both. Therefore, great care must be given to discern whether or not difficulties in a person's life are caused by demonic activity.

Some difficulties may be caused by mental illness or, on rare occasions, by Multiple Personality Disorder (MPD). MPDs often come from traumas of childhood. When this is the case, deliverance is rarely, if ever, called for. Rather, these childhood traumas need to be healed so that the fragmented pieces of the person's life can come back together in order for him or her to be whole.

This is where the gift of discerning of spirits is absolutely essential. Those who minister in this area must do so with great sensitivity to the needs of the person and, if necessary, be willing to seek the help of others who are gifted in deliverance ministry or who are trained professionals.

How, then, can you tell when there is a need for deliverance? Individuals usually know when something is wrong in their lives and they desire to seek help for the condition.

Some persons seeking help may experience:

- Voices urging them to commit suicide or to hurt others.
- Visions or nightmares that convey terror or drive them to do things they would not normally do.
- Bodily contortions that are uncontrollable. This is illustrated in Scripture: "The evil spirit shook the man violently," or "he would cry out and cut himself with stones" (Mark 1:26, 5:5).
- Changes in facial expressions and sound of the voice. A woman's voice may suddenly change to the husky voice of a man, or a man's voice may become very feminine. The tone of voice may also become insulting and vulgar.
- A compulsion to act out with inappropriate behavior.
- Facial expressions and rolling of the eyes with mocking or lustful movements.
- Unpleasant, sulfuric smells in the room or coming from the person's body.
- The room becoming suddenly cold when, in reality, it is warm.
- A driving compulsion to sin.
- Blasphemous thoughts during prayer or worship.
- Confusion when attempting to read and study Scripture.
- Visualizing Jesus doing perverted things.
- Being taken over by some evil power or force.

Some or all of these symptoms may be a good indication of a need for deliverance from demonic influence in a person's life.

Other symptoms that may indicate a need for deliverance are related to attitudes and issues in our lives that control our behavior. Such attitudes are as follows:

- Bitterness
- Resentment
- Hatred
- Fear
- Rage and anger

- Brawling and slander
- Malice

Scriptures instruct us to "Get rid of all bitterness, rage and anger, brawling and slander, along with every form of malice" (Eph. 4:31). When these attitudes are no longer under our control, but are out of control, there is the real possibility that they have become demonic in nature.

Categories of Demonic Activity

It is important to understand the four major categories of unclean or demonic spirits.

- The spirits of sin
- The spirits of trauma
- Ancestral or familiar spirits
- The spirits of the occult

Spirits of Sin

The spirits of sin are characterized by names signifying a human vice or sin. Examples of these are lust, hatred, murder, envy, and other sins that plague a person's life. These represent the sins or weaknesses with which the person is involved. The demonic spirit appears to induce, encourage, and feed upon these sins and weakness. When the demonic spirits are present, it is very difficult for a person to stop committing that particular sin because the demon causes the compulsion for wanting to continue in it. The sin becomes addictive.

Spirits of Trauma

The spirits of trauma bring about the most common need for deliverance. The demonic spirits enter during a time of trauma in a person's life and keep him or her stuck at that point. When a person is wounded by traumas, rejection, fears, or by others sinning against them, unclean spirits can attack through the wounded past. If it is not dealt with, confessed, forgiven, and healed, what begins as an emotional wound can leave a door open to a demonic spirit that will prevent the trauma from being healed.

Much deliverance is aimed at ridding people of various spirits of trauma. Shock, illness, death, accident, incest, and abuse can all leave doors open to this type of spirit. During these times, our normal defenses are let down and an evil spirit can take advantage of our weakened condition and take up residence within us.

It is possible for the demonic spirit to gain subtle entrance in the many grieving experiences of life. Grief finds its source in many places and events:

- a broken relationship
- loss of a loved one to death
- loss of a business or a job
- wounded pride

- a child born out of wedlock
- broken dreams
- miscarriage or barrenness
- disappointment in self
- disillusionment by another
- a feeling that one has been let down by God

Scripture makes it very clear that "heartache crushes the spirit," and "a crushed spirit dries up the bones" (Prov. 15:13, 17:22).

Grieving, especially over the death of a loved one, is natural for a reasonable time. Psychologists say it takes one to three years to be healed from grieving over such a loss. But unresolved, prolonged grief opens the door to spiritual, physical, and emotional problems developing in that person's life.

Unresolved grieving also opens the door to the grieving, weeping, and sorrowing spirits to enter and create difficulty in the healing process. These three spirits will cause us to continue to grieve long after it is time for healing to begin. It is natural to weep for awhile; however, as God's Word declares, "weeping may endure for a night, [time] but joy cometh in the morning" (Ps. 30:5 KJV).

Ancestral or Familiar Spirits

Another category of the demonic is ancestral, or familiar spirits. Ancestral spirits will often have common, familiar, or family names because they take on the identity of persons in our ancestry.

There are two different theories about the nature of ancestral or familiar spirits. The first theory holds they are demonic spirits simply masquerading as the souls of the dead so as to excite people's curiosity about departed relatives. People go to séances to talk to what they think are the spirits of their dead loved ones (as the spirits seem to give information that is familiar only to the family of the deceased).

The second theory is that these ancestral or familiar spirits are truly the spirits of the dead who, for one reason or another, have not been mourned and who are not at rest.

In either case, deliverance can occur as prayer is given to place them in the hands of Jesus. For example, "I command you, [name], to go to Jesus Christ and be sent wherever He would have you go. Jesus will deal with you in His justice, love, and mercy."

Spirits of the Occult

The last category of demonic activity is that of spirits of the occult. Spirits of the occult have unusual personal names: Beelzebub, Pasuzo, or Antichrist. These odd names indicate the spirits are in the higher realms of the evil hierarchy.

Spirits of the occult usually move into people's lives through direct involvement in occult practices. These occult practices include things like, but are not limited to:

- Fortune telling
- Tarot cards

- New Age religious activity
- Channeling of ancient entities
- Following horoscopes
- Satan worship
- Casting magic spells
- Psychic phenomena

These spirits represent a relatively small percentage (perhaps 10 percent) of those encountered. However, they are the most difficult and dangerous in both a person's life and the ministry of deliverance.

Demons of the occult are demons that have entered the person by direct invitation, as they have been involved in occult practices or by parental dedication of the person as a child to Satan. This is the category in which possession by the demonic is the most likely to occur. When this is the case, these individuals should be referred to, or taken to, persons who have experience in the ministry of deliverance. Sources listed in the bibliography are helpful for further study of this occurrence.

The Authority of the Church as the Body of Believers

Jesus considered demons intelligent, evil, powerful, and hostile to humans. However, He gave believers the authority to cast out demons (Luke 9–10). "And these signs will accompany those who believe: In my name they will drive out demons; . . ." (Mark 16:17). That statement establishes the fact that there are demons to be cast out, and the church, as the body of believers, has authority to do it!

We have a Master who is much greater than the world of the demonic: "the one who is in you is greater than the one who is in the world" (1 John 4:4). And that Master is Jesus. He went to the cross to defeat Satan, and He did defeat him: "Since the children have flesh and blood, he too shared in their humanity so that by his death he might destroy him who holds the power of death—that is, the devil . . ." (Heb. 2:14).

Scripture informs us that Jesus has defeated Satan and Satan knows it. We as the church, the body of believers, also need to know it. Otherwise, Satan will continue to make effort to "steal and kill and destroy" (John 10:10).

The church has the authority to be involved in the deliverance ministry of Jesus. He gave the disciples authority to cast out demons.

> *The seventy returned with joy, saying, "Lord, even the demons are subject to us in your name!" And he said to them, "I saw Satan fall like lightning from heaven. Behold, I have given you authority to tread upon serpents and scorpions, and over all the power of the enemy; and nothing shall hurt you."*
>
> —**Luke 10:17–19** RSV

We, as believers, have been given that same authority to deliver persons from bondage to the demonic. We have the authority. We need to know it and know how to use it.

Ministering Deliverance

The Lord's Prayer is the most powerful deliverance prayer available. If you have ever prayed the Lord's Prayer, you have already been involved in deliverance ministry. When the team and the person receiving deliverance pray the prayer together, deliverance happens! "Deliver us from the evil one!" (Matt. 6:13).

Deliverance ministry is a team effort and should always be done by a prayer team that spends time prior to the deliverance ministry in prayer, praise, and thanksgiving to God. It is strongly suggested that deliverance ministry be conducted during daylight hours.

It is important that the ministry team prays for the blood of Jesus to cover and protect the team members, their families, and their possessions, as well as those of the person who is to experience deliverance.

1. As the ministry session begins, the leader of the team speaks to bind Satan and every demonic force that has been sent against this person.

2. The person may be anointed with oil in the sign of the cross and in the name of God the Father, Jesus Christ the Son, and God the Holy Spirit.

3. Instruct the person seeking deliverance that you will be talking with the spirit and not to them. The leader looks the person directly in the eye. It is important that the person keep his or her eyes open so that the unclean spirit is exposed to the light of Jesus' presence through the leader's eyes.

4. The leader then declares that the demons are forbidden to communicate with one another, draw strength from one another, or accomplish the purpose for which they were sent. They are also forbidden to manifest themselves in any way. This is important, as demons love to make a display of themselves as they leave. We have the authority to not allow it to happen.

5. Jesus is the Deliverer, and it is important for the team to seek Jesus' direction and let Him identify the "strong man," (the name of the spirit) and give the way in which it is to be cast out. When Jesus was talking about driving out demons by the Spirit of God, He said, "Or again, how can anyone enter a strong man's house and carry off his possessions unless he first ties up the strong man?" (Matt. 12:29). Jesus knows the strong man as well as the stronghold—the mind-set that accompanies the need for deliverance.

6. The leader will then command the demonic spirit to leave in the name of Jesus. For example, "[*Name of the spirit*], I command you to leave. This is the dwelling place of the Holy Spirit, and you cannot stay here."

7. Tell the person to participate in the deliverance by telling the unclean spirit to leave, for often the demonic spirit will say that the person does not want them to leave.

8. Watch the person's actions to see if there is a yawn, sigh, cough, relaxation, peace, or light in the eyes. These may all be signs of the demon leaving.

9. Test questions may be asked to validate the deliverance. These may include questions like:

    - Do you joyfully confess Jesus Christ to be Lord and Savior, having come in the flesh as the only Redeemer of all humankind?

    - Do you acknowledge that Satan is a false god, a liar, a deceiver, the prince of darkness?

    - Do you forsake all loyalty and allegiance to Satan?

10. Ask the person how he or she feels. Is there still heaviness, oppression, fear, or anything that does not seem right? If so, then continue seeking God's guidance for what remains to be done.

    If the person acknowledges that there is a positive difference and that there is a sense of freedom or quiet or peace, then encourage him or her to walk in the deliverance through the celebration of Holy Communion. Often, a person cannot receive the sacrament if an unclean spirit is still present, but joyfully receives it if the spirit is gone.

11. The person is then encouraged to make a new commitment to Jesus, to be filled with the Holy Spirit, and to seek a release of the Holy Spirit's power in his or her life.

12. The deliverance session should end with a prayer of thanksgiving and an encouragement for the person to be in praise and thanksgiving to God for at least a week as a way of accepting and celebrating the time of deliverance.

Aftercare is a vital part of deliverance. The team must keep in touch with the person who has experienced deliverance and place him or her under the care of a strong, mature Christian for ongoing oversight.

Persons who have been delivered from the demonic are often weary because they have gone through a spiritual battle. It is important to monitor their lives and encourage them to rest, to be in Scripture, to praise and sing, and to have fellowship with a Christian support group.

They will need to learn to walk in the Light, for they have been transferred out of the kingdom of darkness into the kingdom of light. They will need to be reminded that:

You are a chosen people, a royal priesthood, a holy nation, a people belonging to God, that you may declare the praises of him who called you out of darkness into his wonderful light.
—1 Peter 2:9

A major portion of Jesus' ministry involved deliverance of some kind. He delivered people out of ignorance into understanding: "The true light that gives light [enlightens] to every man was coming into the world" (John 1:9). He delivered them from sickness to health: "and all who touched him were healed" (Matt. 14:36). He also delivered people from the demonic: "he rebuked the evil spirit. 'You deaf and mute spirit,' he said, 'I command you, come out of him and never enter him again'" (Mark 9:25).

Those who are in Jesus' ministry today will also be involved in a ministry of helping persons move from ignorance to understanding, from sickness to health, and from bondage in the demonic to freedom. In doing so they, along with the one receiving deliverance, will be engaged in spiritual warfare. This necessitates drawing on the power of God's Holy Spirit for the work of ministry, but also requires a time of rest and restoration following the deliverance.

It is the work of the Holy Spirit to set the captive free!

IDEAS FOR REFLECTION

Please share at a level that is comfortable for you.

1. What does Scripture teach about Satan and demons?
2. What are some of the attributes of the character of Satan?
3. What do you think of when you hear the word "deliverance" as related to healing?
4. Do you believe that demons or unclean spirits are present-day realities? If so, why? If not, why not?
5. What has been your experience in relating to persons whose lives may have been affected by demonic powers?
6. Are you aware of persons who may be involved in the occult and have need for deliverance?
7. Do you feel that God has enabled you to discern if and when a person may be influenced by unclean spirits?
8. What are some of the ways by which you may differentiate between a person's need for deliverance or for counseling and healing of emotional hurts?
9. What would you do in order to help a person readjust to his or her new lifestyle after having been delivered from the demonic?
10. How may persons protect themselves from being harassed by the demonic?

XIII. PHYSICAL HEALING

This chapter will be a study of the various kinds and levels of physical healings that may be expected and anticipated as prayers are offered for those who are ill.

Among the spiritual gifts manifested by the Holy Spirit in the body of Christ is the "gifts of healings" (1 Cor. 12:9). There are, indeed, various kinds of healings that are experienced.

There are different theologies regarding healing and the part that God plays in it. Some include:

- God never healed.

- God used to do that, but doesn't do it any longer.

- God will do things like that in the future.

- God is the same yesterday, today and forever; therefore, God healed in the past, God heals in the present, and God will continue to heal into the future.

THE TRUTH IS, GOD HEALS!

SCRIPTURE:

As soon as they left the synagogue, they went with James and John to the home of Simon and Andrew. Simon's mother-in-law was in bed with a fever, and they told Jesus about her. So he went to her, took her hand and helped her up. The fever left her and she began to wait on them. That evening after sunset the people brought to Jesus all the sick and demon-possessed. The whole town gathered at the door, and Jesus healed many who had various diseases. He also drove out many demons, but he would not let the demons speak because they knew who he was.
—**Mark 1:29–34**

A man with leprosy came to him and begged him on his knees, "If you are willing, you can make me clean." Filled with compassion, Jesus reached out his hand and touched the man. "I am willing," he said. "Be clean!" Immediately the leprosy left him and he was cured.
—**Mark 1:40–42**

. . . to another faith by the same Spirit, to another gifts of healing by that one Spirit . . .
—**1 Corinthians 12:9**

Additional Scripture Readings: Mark 1:21–28, 35–39; 1: 43–2:17; James 5:13–16

During the course of Jesus' life and ministry here on earth, He was engaged in a redemption ministry. He came to redeem humanity. That redemption is expressed in many ways.

Jesus' ministry involved two major thrusts: (1) He preached the kingdom of God, the good news of God's love for humanity, and (2) He healed the sick. *He preached the kingdom of God and healed the sick.* In many cases, He preached the kingdom of God *by* healing the sick. He demonstrated the good news about which He spoke. Healing was not incidental to His mission. It was basic. Scripture records that a major portion of Jesus' ministry involved healing of some kind. Scripture also reveals that Jesus was concerned with seeing the individual as a whole person—spirit, soul, body, and relationships. He healed persons in all areas of their lives.

Jesus was involved with bringing about the healing of one's spirit. He forgave sins and brought reconciliation between persons and God, between persons with other persons, and between a person and him or herself.

Jesus brought healing to emotions and released people from spiritual powers which gripped their lives and held their minds captive.

He delivered people from imprisonment to demonic forces.

He healed the physical body, releasing persons from disease, sickness, brokenness, blindness, deafness, speechlessness, and death. He healed the maimed, the lame, and those with severe pain (Matt. 15:29–31).

He spoke, taught, and healed with authority, as one who was able to bring about that which He spoke: forgiveness, deliverance, and healing.

He gave the authority to heal to His disciples, and through the indwelling presence of the Holy Spirit, that same power and authority is available to the church today. The church now becomes the healed and the healing community for this present world (Acts 1:4–8).

Healing involves every part of our human makeup: spirit, soul, body and relationships. In his letter to the Corinthian church, the apostle Paul lists the gifts of the Holy Spirit. Included in that list is the "gifts of healings" (1 Cor. 12:9). The word "gifts" indicates that there is more than one kind of healing. There are at least five kinds and three levels of healing. In addition, there is need for deliverance from those attitudes, behavior patterns, or negative influences that keep our lives in bondage to that which could destroy us.

Kinds of Healings

There are five kinds of healings. The primary healing, and one that is essential to all our other healing and wholeness, is the healing of our human spirit.

The Human Spirit

The first kind of healing has to do with the human spirit as diseased by sin. Sin is that which keeps us separated, alienated, and estranged from God, our Creator, the Source of our health and wholeness. To be healed in our spirit is to be in right relationship with God.

Human Emotions

The second kind of healing has to do with our emotions. Emotional hurts, traumas, and those other things related to our will and thought life often keep us from being the persons God has intended for us to be.

Relationships

The third healing has to do with our relationships. It is important to our well-being that we be in right relationship with others around us through forgiveness and reconciliation. This was Jesus' ministry. "For God was pleased to have all his fullness dwell in him [Jesus], and through him to reconcile to himself all things . . ." (Col. 1:19–20).

Consequently, we have been given the ministry of reconciliation—bringing people into right relationship with God and with other people: "All this is from God, who reconciled us to himself through Christ and gave us the ministry of reconciliation" (2 Cor. 5:18).

Deliverance

The fourth kind of healing is deliverance. Deliverance involves freedom from bondage to those forces that would keep us in darkness, ignorance, hatred, and bitterness.

It is a healing that brings us out of the kingdom of darkness into the kingdom of light, out of bondage into freedom, out from the lie into the truth, and out from death into life.

Physical Healing

The fifth kind of healing has to do with our physical bodies. We live in a world wherein there is sickness, accident, disease, suffering, pain, and death. It is a reality with which we are faced each day.

Vast amounts of financial resources are spent annually in a search for physical wholeness and well-being. It is the desire of the human heart to be whole in spirit, mind, body, and relationships, and to be delivered from those things that would destroy us.

God, in His great mercy and love, has provided ways for those healings to happen. Healing is a part of God's gift to creation as an expression of His love.

Levels of Healing

There are levels of healing that help us to better understand the diverse ways in which God moves upon our lives, enabling us to experience health and wholeness.

Natural Healing

Natural healing is designed into our creation and, in fact, into the life of all living cells.

Plant, animal, and human life all experience natural healing—a healing process that appears to be a standard part of virtually all forms of living beings and things.

The natural healing process functions even though we may not be aware of it and generally are not. For example, when a finger is cut, instantly the healing process begins. The body bleeds to cleanse the wound, and the white cells and platelets rush to the cut and begin their work of protecting the body against invasion by germs and bacteria. They work to close the wound, forming a protective scab to guard against infection. New skin develops under the scab and soon it is difficult to see where the skin had been cut. If the injury was severe, the scar becomes stronger than the original skin. The scar is the sign of a healed wound.

The same natural healing process is true of bones, clogged veins, arteries, and organs. The body works to heal itself. It is part of the design put together by God.

The psalmist describes how we are fearfully and wonderfully made: "For you created my inmost being; you knit me together in my mother's womb. I praise you because I am fearfully and wonderfully made . . ." (Ps. 139:13–14).

Natural healing takes place whether or not we are aware of it, whether or not we assist in its occurrence, or whether or not we acknowledge any divine source involved.

Natural healing is a merciful gift from God. Like rain, it comes to the just and the unjust, the wicked and the righteous, the good and the bad, the grateful and the ungrateful.

Natural healing is the dependable principle used by medical science in its work.

Healing that Requires Help

There are times when the body cannot heal itself; the mind cannot heal itself; and the spirit cannot heal itself. They need help.

The wound, trauma, hurt, or other insult to the person is so severe, it must have help to be made whole. For the Christian, prayer is the primary and greatest aid to bring about healing, for it puts the person in need in touch with the God who heals.

In addition to prayer, modern medical science plays a major role in the healing of our bodies. However, in our western culture, there is a tendency to assign physical healing to medical science alone. Specialization is generally our approach to healing.

This is incomplete. Remember the variety of help available to facilitate healing includes prayer, homeopathy, medical assistance, therapy, caregiving, and other means by which healing may occur.

The medical profession is usually geared toward assisting the natural healing processes in the body to fulfill their function.

Psychiatrists are doctors trained to assist the natural healing processes in the body and mind, or psyche, to fulfill their function, focusing primarily on the mind.

People in the spiritual professions assist the natural healing processes in the human spirit to fulfill their function. Though humans have a natural bent to sinning, there is also an innate desire (put there by God) to be in right relationship with the Creator.

Each profession strives in its area of expertise to make people healthy in the spirit, mind, and body.

However, it is important to not become so specialized that we treat the different facets of our lives as though they were not related to the others. We are whole beings, and what affects the body affects the mind and also the spirit. Likewise, whatever affects the mind also affects the spirit and the body. Whatever affects the spirit also affects the body and the mind, for all are inextricably bound together.

More and more people in the helping professions are realizing that we are essentially unified beings with all facets of our lives interrelated. True holistic healing takes into account the trinitarian nature of the human being—spirit, soul, and body—knowing that each facet affects the other.

Surgeries, medications, and therapies are all parts of the healing process and are recognized by a major part of the Christian community as gifts from God.

Supernatural Healing

A third level of healing has to do with a supernatural move of God to touch and heal the human body. When God sovereignly heals, He uses processes and laws with which we are not familiar and brings about results that we are unable to accomplish. God's thoughts and ways are beyond our comprehension. As the Word of God states: "'For my thoughts are not your thoughts, neither are your ways my ways,' declares the Lord" (Isa. 55:8).

We cannot always understand the ways of God when it comes to physical healing. There is a mystery that surrounds the relationship between God and creation; nevertheless, God chooses to reveal His ways much of the time.

Healing cannot be reduced to a formula, a methodology, a prescription, or a technique. Supernatural healing is a sovereign intervention of God's Holy Spirit. God moves in sovereign ways to heal in all of creation—whether or not that creation acknowledges God as the Healer.

Often, God moves sovereignly to heal in direct response to prayer offered by persons of faith on behalf of one who is ill.

> *And these signs will follow those who believe . . . they will lay hands on the sick, and they will recover.*
>
> —**Mark 16:17–18** NKJV

Whether through the natural healing process, medical science, prayer, or through the sovereign hand of God, God is to be acknowledged as our Healer and the One who makes us whole in spirit, soul, and body.

God is the One who keeps the promise, "I am the Lord that healeth thee" (Exod. 15:26 KJV).

IDEAS FOR REFLECTION

Please share at a level that is comfortable for you.

1. Explore in Scripture how Jesus had a concern for the whole person: spirit, mind, body, and relationships. Discuss Matthew 4:23–24; Mark 1:40–45, 2:1–12; Luke 8:40–56; John 7:23.

2. As it is comfortable for you, share a time when you have experienced natural healing taking place in your own body.

3. How have you experienced healing in your body through the aid of professional helpers such as physicians, therapists, medications, or counseling?

4. How have you experienced, or witnessed in the life of another, healing through prayer?

5. Share how you have experienced, or witnessed in the life of another, the sovereign move of God to bring healing to a person.

6. Do you believe that healing is still a part of the ministry of the church? Why or why not?

XIV. THE PHYSICAL HEALING PROCESS

Now let's consider a healing process from the Christian perspective, some ways in which healing happens, and what is the ultimate healing for the Christian.

It is important to understand that faith plays an important part in the healing process: "Now faith is the assurance of things hoped for, the conviction of things not seen" (Heb. 11:1 RSV).

Christians believe that the name of Jesus carries with it the power and authority to bring healing and the power and authority to help others experience healing. Faith coupled with hope—which is absolute confidence and trust in God—releases the power of God to work miracles in our lives.

SCRIPTURE:

Now when Jesus returned, a crowd welcomed him, for they were all expecting him. Then a man named Jairus, a ruler of the synagogue, came and fell at Jesus' feet, pleading with him to come to his house because his only daughter, a girl of about twelve, was dying. As Jesus was on his way, the crowds almost crushed him. And a woman was there who had been subject to bleeding for twelve years, but no one could heal her. She came up behind him and touched the edge of his cloak, and immediately her bleeding stopped. "Who touched me?" Jesus asked. When they all denied it, Peter said, "Master, the people are crowding and pressing against you." But Jesus said, "Someone touched me; I know that power has gone out from me." Then the woman, seeing that she could not go unnoticed, came trembling and fell at his feet. In the presence of all the people, she told why she had touched him and how she had been instantly healed. Then he said to her, "Daughter, your faith has healed you. Go in peace." While Jesus was still speaking, someone came from the house of Jairus, the synagogue ruler. "Your daughter is dead," he said. "Don't bother the teacher any more." Hearing this, Jesus said to Jairus, "Don't be afraid; just believe, and she will be healed." When he arrived at the house of Jairus, he did not let anyone go in with him except Peter, John and James, and the child's father and mother. Meanwhile, all the people were wailing and mourning for her. "Stop wailing," Jesus said. "She is not dead but asleep." They laughed at him, knowing that she was dead. But he took her by the hand and said, "My child, get up!" Her spirit returned, and at once she stood up. Then Jesus told them to give her something to eat. Her parents were astonished, but he ordered them not to tell anyone what had happened.

—Luke 8:40–56

Additional Scripture Readings: Mark 2:1–12

God provided ways by which we may participate in the healing process and experience wholeness in our bodies—as well as our minds and spirits.

A Process for Healing

There is a process by which we may assist healing to take place in all areas of our lives, including our physical healing. Each step is important and must be carefully considered by the one desiring to be whole.

Confession

Confession allows us to acknowledge the reality and truth of the condition in which we find ourselves.

Whether the condition is related to spiritual, emotional, or physical needs, it is important to recognize that the condition is real. One cannot pretend that it does not exist or that it does not matter.

The person who experiences serious physical symptoms must never pass them off as being nothing or having no importance. To deny the presence of a disease or physical malady is to court disaster in the body.

To confess the condition has nothing to do with negative confession—that is, bringing sickness on ourselves by saying we are sick. Rather, it is to acknowledge the reality of its presence. To confess the truth is to open the door to receive real help for the condition.

To state the truth: "I have been diagnosed with cancer," "I have a tumor," "I have ulcers," "I have a problem with alcohol," or "I am plagued by a particular sin," is to take the first step toward healing and wholeness.

Repentance

There are two types of repentance.

- Metanoia: metanoia means "deep repentance." It means to grieve over personal responsibility for bringing about the condition, if that is, indeed, the case.

- The second type of repentance is to rethink. It means to think again about personal involvement in a lifestyle that fosters bad health—if that is, indeed, the case.

Many times we suffer physical maladies simply because we have disobeyed basic health laws, abused use of drugs, became involved in sexual promiscuity, or ignored rules of safety, and our bodies experience the consequences. Much illness directly results from our willful disobedience of God's good health laws.

It is important to rethink our attitudes and adjust those habits that do not contribute to healthy bodies.

Forgiveness

Sometimes we need to seek God's forgiveness for the lifestyle, attitudes, or behavior patterns that have contributed to the condition of our physical bodies.

Our dietary habits, our work and rest routines, our personal hygiene, and our general demeanor play a major part in opening the door for sickness to invade our bodies. We need to examine ourselves and seek God's forgiveness for the poor care we give to God's temple, our bodies.

Pray for Healing

We are instructed in Scripture to pray for one another:

> *Is any one of you sick? He should call the elders of the church to pray over him and anoint him with oil in the name of the Lord. And the prayer offered in faith will make the sick person well; the Lord will raise him up. If he has sinned, he will be forgiven. Therefore confess your sins to each other and pray for each other so that you may be healed. The prayer of a righteous man is powerful and effective.*
>
> —James 5:14–16

Prayer creates that relationship with God that releases healing power to the needs of the person seeking healing.

When praying for another, we are not alone; we are working in concert with God's Holy Spirit. Therefore, it is important to seek God's direction as to how to pray for those who come for healing. "God, how would you have me pray for this loved one?" Then, listen and pray according to the leading of God's Holy Spirit.

Often, the Lord will lead the one in prayer ministry to anoint the sick person with oil, lay hands on him or her, and pray for the person (James 5:14).

Two Ways to Pray: Once God has given the direction for prayer, understand that we may pray one of two ways or with a combination of the two:

- The first way to pray is to **command**. When sure of God's direction, we may command the physical malady to leave the body, for bones to knit, for muscles to be strong, for cells to be restored. Living cells respond to command. Example: "Tumor [*or whatever malady*], I command you in the name of Jesus, leave this body." "Pain, in the name of Jesus, leave."

- The second way to pray is to **ask**. It is also appropriate to ask Jesus to heal and fill the person with His healing presence. It is never appropriate to command Jesus to do anything! For example: "Jesus, we ask you to fill this person with Your powerful healing presence. We ask You to remove the tumor, renew this body, and make him or her whole. We ask this in Your name. Amen."

Persons who are in need of prayer for healing often seek out help. We do not have to seek them out. When they come for healing prayer, they are expressing their faith that God is able to heal them, and then we make ourselves available to pray for them.

The privacy of persons seeking ministry must be respected. **Confidentiality is absolutely essential when praying for another.** If a person's story is to be told, they must tell it or give permission for it to be shared by another.

Experience Healing

After praying for healing for someone, it is helpful to ask the person to test the healing, that is, to see if there is any change in the condition. This may be done by moving arms, legs, torso, hips, etc., to see if any healing was experienced.

Ask questions such as, "How do you feel?" "Do you feel 25 percent better? 50 percent better? 10 percent better?" It is important to focus on that which has been accomplished and not on that which has not yet been accomplished.

We give thanks to God for what He is doing, not complain about that which God has not yet done.

A word must be said here about "claiming a healing," or saying that a person is healed when there is no indication that healing has indeed happened. A healing should be "claimed" only if the healing is real. If healed, praise God for the healing. If not yet healed, continue to pray, and praise God for working toward that healing and for grace that sustains while healing is in process.

If persons are on medication or in braces, encourage them to go to their physicians to have the braces removed or be told they no longer need medication. This will be a testimony to the health-care person—as per Jesus' instruction to the leper in Mark 1:40–45. The leper's healing would be a testimony to the priests as to the healing power of God in Jesus. A present-day healing would, in a similar way, be testimony to health-care professions.

Some healings are obvious and need no medical confirmation, as with Matthew's witness to the lame walking, the blind seeing, and the deaf hearing (Matt. 4:23–24).

Ways in which Healing Happens

Healing happens in a variety of ways, but God is always at the center of the healing process.

Rapid Healing

There are times when God moves powerfully, sovereignly, and quickly to bring healing. Many whom Jesus touched were healed immediately.

Sometimes people are healed during the course of the prayer that is said on their behalf. It is appropriate to give glory to God and then the healing becomes a vital part of the person's testimony to the goodness of God.

God, and not the person praying, is the one who receives the glory for the healing. It is the person's responsibility to pray, and it is God's power that heals.

Gradual Healing

Healing may not always happen quickly, but over time and gradually. A person may not be healed immediately but may be healed in a few days or a few months.

Jesus touched the eyes of a blind man and then asked him if he could see. He said that he could see men, but they looked like trees walking. Jesus then touched him a second time, and he was able to see clearly (Mark 8:22–26).

When healing is slower in coming, it is appropriate to continue praying, giving praise to God for working the miracle of healing, and to thank God for the grace that sustains through the healing process.

In the case of prolonged illness, prayer teams may be organized to provide soaking prayer for the person who is ill. There are several ways this may be done. One way soaking prayer occurs is when a small team of three or four persons gathers with the person daily or weekly at a time convenient for the person and lays hands on the sick person, anoints him or her with oil, seeks God's direction, and prays accordingly.

No Apparent Healing

It remains a mystery as to why some are healed and some are not, especially when fervent prayers are said for healing. This should not discourage believers from praying for and expecting healing.

Not all are healed through medical science, yet people continue to seek healing through medicines and therapies.

Not all are healed through counseling treatment, yet people continue to receive counseling toward healing.

Not all are healed through prayer, yet people continue to pray for healing, believing that the God of our Lord Jesus Christ is the God who heals.

The human body ultimately dies, either because of age, disease, accident, or unknown causes. Death is a part of the life process. All that lives, dies. Yet, death is not the end for the Christian.

Death is *not* the ultimate healing. New Testament teaching on the subject of death makes this very clear. Death may bring about release from painful suffering and prolonged distress; however, it is not a healing.

Death is the wages of sin.

> *For the wages of sin is death, but the gift of God is eternal life in Christ Jesus our Lord.*
> —**Romans 6:23**

Death is a stronghold of the adversary.

> *Since the children have flesh and blood, he too shared in their humanity so that by his death he might destroy him who holds the power of death—that is, the devil—and free those who all their lives were held in slavery by their fear of death.*
> —**Hebrews 2:14–15**

Jesus came to destroy death.

> *This grace [God's] was given us in Christ Jesus before the beginning of time, but it has now been revealed through the appearing of our Savior, Christ Jesus, who has destroyed death and has brought life and immortality to light through the gospel.*
> —**2 Timothy 1:9–10**

Death is swallowed up in victory.

> *When the perishable has been clothed with the imperishable, and the mortal with immortality, then the saying that is written will come true: "Death has been swallowed up in victory.*

Where, O death, is your victory? Where, O death, is your sting?" The sting of death is sin, and the power of sin is the law. But thanks be to God! He gives us the victory through our Lord Jesus Christ.

—1 Corinthians 15:54–57

Death is ultimately destroyed.

The last enemy to be destroyed is death.

—1 Corinthians 15:26

Then death and Hades were thrown into the lake of fire.

—Revelations 20:1–4, paraphrased

The Ultimate Healing Is in the Resurrection

Jesus said to Martha, at the occasion of the death of Lazarus, "I am the resurrection and the life. He who believes in me will live, even though he dies; and whoever lives and believes in me will never die" (John 11:25–26).

When Jesus had heard about Lazarus's illness, he said in part, "This sickness will not end in death" (John 11:4).

Lazarus did, in fact, die. By the time Jesus returned to Bethany, Lazarus had been in the grave four days. However, it did not end there. Jesus raised him from the dead, and it ended in a resurrection from the dead.

The believer is one who already enjoys eternal life, even in the here and now. Jesus defines eternal life in His prayer that is recorded in John: "Now this is eternal life: that they may know you, the only true God, and Jesus Christ, whom you have sent" (17:3). Even though the body is ill and may cease to function, life shall not cease for the believer.

Those who minister to the sick and dying have good news to share with them. You can say to them, "Your sickness will not end in death. You can trust the promise of Jesus that those who believe in him will never die."

Those who are facing a life-threatening sickness must be helped to realize that theirs is an illness that will not end in death. It ends in the resurrection. *The ultimate healing is in the resurrection!*

The resurrection of Jesus Christ from the dead stands at the heart and core of the Christian faith. It is the pivotal event that separates the Christian way of life from all other religions. The declaration of the church from the beginning summarized the faith that separates the Christian faith from all other faiths. "Christ has died! Christ is risen! Christ will come again!"

Death has been conquered and Christ's promise of eternal life for those who believe in Him has become a reality.

Thus, as people of faith and followers of Jesus, our sickness, whatever it may be, will not end in death. It will end in the resurrection and eternal life.

IDEAS FOR REFLECTION

Please share at a level that is comfortable for you.

1. Should the church be involved in a healing ministry or leave that in the hands of professional and skilled medical people?

2. What should the church body do when members are ill?

3. What would be the first thing you would do if asked to pray for someone who is ill?

4. Do the prayers of righteous people help to bring healing to others?

5. How important is confession to our spiritual, emotional, and physical health?

6. Do you feel that forgiveness is important in the need for physical healing?

7. When faced with a life-threatening disease, how should one pray?

8. How do you feel about the fact that some people are healed rapidly, while others remain ill for longer periods of time, while yet others appear to not receive healing?

9. Discuss the various steps in the process for healing and make application to personal experiences with yourself or with others who have been ill.

WORKSHOP ON PRAYER FOR HEALING

This workshop provides directions for an opportunity to receive ministry for healing and to minister to others.

1. **The workshop will begin with the facilitator praying for the entire gathering.**

2. **Following the prayer, move into groups of three.**

3. **One person in each group will share his or her prayer need.**

    Confess the malady. Do not go into great detail about its history. State simply, in twenty-five words or less, the condition that is being experienced. For example: "I have pain in my lower back." "I have a sprained ankle." "I have trouble hearing." "I want to see." "I have cancer in my lungs."

4. **The two remaining persons become the prayer team.**

    Seek God's direction as to how to pray, and then pray as you are led by the Holy Spirit, following some of the guidelines discussed previously. Remember, however, healing comes by the power and working of the Holy Spirit, not by method used.

5. **Test the healing.**

    You might ask, "How do you feel now?", "Is the pain better?", or similar questions. Ask the person receiving prayer to do something physically that they couldn't before.

6. **After completing prayer with the first person, the second person will share** with the remaining two, who become the prayer team. Follow the same procedure as with the first prayer.

7. **When all have had prayer and have been able to pray for another, join hands and** give praise to God for what has been done. Example: "I want to praise God for the way in which I have been blessed by this prayer group." "I praise God for the healing I have received."

8. **Since this is the last session of the series, it may conclude** with everyone in the group having opportunity to share how their lives have been impacted by God during this series of study. How they have:

    a. Experienced personal healing in body, mind, or spirit.

    b. Gained new ways in which to minister to others.

    c. Become more comfortable in sharing with others.

    d. Gained better understanding of the church's role in healing ministry.

9. **Close the session in prayer.**

APPENDIX

Facilitator's Guide for *Anointed to Heal*
A Study Guide for Healing and Wholeness from a Christian Perspective

Teaching Chapter I
"GOD IS OUR COMFORTER"

NOTE: Facilitators are highly encouraged to read and study resource materials listed in the bibliography of this book. They are also encouraged to take advantage of available training events and seminars related to the subject of healing and wholeness, thereby providing more effective leadership for the class participants.

Open the session with prayer:

"Gracious and loving God, God of our Lord, Jesus Christ, we pray for the guidance of Your Holy Spirit as we enter this time of study. Be our Teacher, our Counselor, and our Guide so that we may discover a new and deeper knowledge and understanding of who You are and how we may come into a closer walk with You. Renew us and remake us into the image of Jesus, Your Son, in whose name we pray. Amen."

Read aloud the session's introductory statement.

Read the related Scripture passage(s).

This first session is divided into two parts and may be used as two different sessions if desired. The facilitator may seek response and discussion from the class on each of the subjects, "God Is Our Comforter" and "The God to Whom We Pray." These two topics lay the groundwork upon which the subject of healing is based.

The first part of the session, "God Is Our Comforter," is designed to help students understand that God is for us and not against us. The second part of the session, "The God to Whom We Pray," reminds us that God is present at all times, in all places, and in all circumstances to hear and respond to our prayers. God's presence surrounds us with knowledge that enlightens our thinking and love that embraces us in the circumstances in which we find ourselves.

It is recommended that each of the subtopics be discussed separately. That is, the facilitator first teaches on "God Is Our Comforter" and leads members to respond, followed by discussion related to the subtopic, "The God to Whom We Pray."

In addition to the questions in the reflection section at the end of the chapter, the facilitator may wish to include the following:

- What is your understanding of the holiness of God?
- How is it possible for God's holiness to be shown in an individual's life?
- How does the holiness of God affect our personal prayer life?
- What part does God's holiness play in our praying for others?
- The class members may also discuss how this concept of holiness affects their personal prayer life.

This process may be repeated for the other characteristics of the nature of God: Spirit, Consuming Fire, Light, and Love.

ALTERNATIVE: The facilitator may instruct on all five characteristics of the nature of God, then have members of the class respond with discussion and/or questions relative to that which is of special importance to them.

The facilitator will want to establish the primary truth that:

- God is our Creator, not our Destroyer.
- Jesus is our Advocate, not our Adversary.
- The Holy Spirit is our Comforter, not our Afflicter.

Close the session with prayer.

The prayer may be spontaneous or written. For example, you might pray: "Gracious and loving God, the source of life and the giver of every good and perfect gift, we thank You that You are a God of compassion and have come to be with us in Jesus and through Your indwelling Holy Spirit. We thank You for being the Holy God who cleanses, purifies, and empowers our lives for abundant living.

"We give thanks for Your Holy Spirit who is our Teacher and who leads us into the way of truth. In the name of Jesus we pray. Amen."

Teaching Chapter II
"SOURCES OF AFFLICTION"

Open the session with prayer.

Read aloud the session's introductory statement.

Read the related Scripture passage(s).

Have the class read or the facilitator present the subject of pain and the part it plays in the healing process. Talk about suffering being "pain out of control." Perhaps class members have experienced this kind of suffering.

Discuss the facets of suffering that we may not understand. Suffering has the dimension of mystery related to it. How does that element of mystery affect our understanding of the goodness of God?

When the subject of disobedience is presented, allow class members to respond to each area in which suffering is experienced and give personal illustrations, such as how the breaking of

God's spiritual laws resulted in personal suffering. The same may be repeated for each of the other laws and resulting suffering. This approach allows the class to personally identify with suffering and not view it from a purely intellectual perspective.

When presenting material related to the root causes of suffering, allow time for class members to respond to the concept that Satan is a root cause of human suffering. Class members will have different understandings of the reality of Satan. This will have impact on the topic of deliverance discussed later.

Encourage participants to discuss how they have experienced suffering as a result of making an effort to be obedient to God's laws. They should share as it is comfortable.

Use the same approach as the class discusses circumstances, such as illness, accident, etc., which brought suffering and pain into their lives.

Use the questions at the end of the chapter as a guide for the discussion period.

Close the session with prayer.

Teaching Chapter III
"GOD COMFORTS US IN OUR AFFLICTION"

Open the session with prayer.

Read aloud the session's introductory statement.

Read the related Scripture passage(s).

Work through the Scriptures that illustrate various dimensions of suffering. Have class members use their Bibles.

Following this Bible research, help the class members understand that part of our work as the body of Christ is to minister to others who have needs in any area of their lives. In doing so, we follow the example of Jesus as He ministered healing and wholeness to others.

Follow the questions in the discussion guide as you work through the material for this session.

Close the session by having class members pray for one another.

Sample Prayer:

"Heavenly Father, I ask that You touch [*name*'s] life and bring comfort to the area of pain in his/her life. Thank You for knowing the situation and the way to bring healing to it. Restore the joy of Your salvation and renew strength in his/her life. I ask this in Jesus' name. Amen."

Teaching Chapter IV
"THE HOLY SPIRIT—GOD'S PROMISED GIFT"

Open the session with prayer.

Read aloud up to the section headed "Who Is the Holy Spirit." Emphasize the importance of the work of God's Holy Spirit in the ministry of healing and wholeness. It is the power of the Holy Spirit that enables effective ministry to happen.

Make sure that study participants have time and opportunity to discuss the materials related to the questions, "Who is the Holy Spirit?" and "What is the work of the Holy Spirit?"

Ask. What is your response to the statement that "the Holy Spirit is not a third god, nor is the Holy Spirit one-third of God?"

Let individuals have time to think about this and respond—always keeping in mind the concluding statement that the Holy Spirit IS God.

Have participants discuss ways in which they have experienced the Holy Spirit working in their life experiences as:

- Encourager
- Teacher
- Counselor/Advisor
- Truth Revealer
- Convicter of something that is wrong
- Giver of direction

Close the session with prayer.

Teaching Chapter V
"BAPTISM AND THE HOLY SPIRIT"

Open the session with prayer.

Read the related Scripture passage(s).

Begin the discussion by asking:

How many of you have been water baptized? Would you be comfortable sharing the circumstances of that baptism? Were you an infant, a youth, or an adult? Were you baptized in church or in another setting, such as a lake or river?

Jesus told His disciples that they would be baptized with the Holy Spirit (Acts 1:5). Ask: How many of you have experienced being baptized with the Holy Spirit and would you be comfortable sharing the circumstances of that baptism?

Discuss how you have experienced the Holy Spirit:

- leading you into a relationship with Jesus?
- cleaning up areas of your life and changing your behavior?
- developing spiritual fruit in your life?
- releasing spiritual gifts in your life?

Give opportunity for those who desire to be baptized with the Holy Spirit to have that experience at this time.

Pray together the prayer at the end of chapter V, then close the time with a prayer of thanksgiving.

Teaching Chapter VI
"THE WORD OF KNOWLEDGE"

Open the session with prayer.

Introduce the session by reading up to the heading "Kinds of Knowledge." Give group opportunity to discuss the kinds of tools they use in their everyday or professional lives. This will help participants understand the makeup of the members of the group and also help them identify spiritual gifts as tools that God has given them for ministry.

Facilitate discussion of the various levels of knowledge:

- Natural
- Eternal
- Word of Knowledge

Ask "How have you experienced each of these levels of knowledge functioning in your life?"

Discuss the various ways in which God speaks and how they have experienced this in their lives.

Give plenty of time for the group to engage in the workshop that enables them to listen to God for direction on how to pray for each other. Follow the directions for the workshop provided at the end of chapter VI.

Close the discussion and workshop time with prayer.

Teaching Chapter VII
"HEALING THE HUMAN SPIRIT"

Open the session with prayer.

Read aloud the session's introductory statement.

Luke 4:18–19 is the primary Scripture for this session. It was the inauguration of Jesus' public ministry and set the direction in which He would go in proclaiming the good news and bringing healing and wholeness to people. Through His choice of this Scripture passage from Isaiah 61, Jesus demonstrated the nature of His ministry and the kingdom of God.

Discuss the concept that persons are spirit, soul, body, and relationships, not spirit *and* soul *and* body.

Help class members understand the nature and consequences of sin and the part it plays in causing persons to have a diseased spirit.

Discuss the symptoms that are stated in the chapter and how they impact the eyes, personal countenance, negative attitudes, and self-righteousness. Class members may think of other symptoms, some of which may be present in their own lives.

Treatment of the diseased spirit is based on developing a wholesome relationship with God. Emphasize that the Holy Spirit plays the essential role in healing the human spirit and in the healing of the whole person. Also, give careful study to the holy disciplines of prayer, study of Scripture, and worship as they also play a major part in other areas of healing.

Exercise

Use the list on page 53 to lead the class in an exercise that will be helpful as they minister to others who have need of spiritual healing.

Get class members into groups of three. These will be prayer/ministry teams. One will share, following the process below, while the other two members minister according to steps two through five. When the first person is finished, follow the same process with person two, then three, until all have had opportunity to give and receive prayer.

1. Have individuals acknowledge, as is comfortable for them, a condition in their spirit (relationship with God) that needs healing. Confess sin that is present.

2. Direct them to seek God's forgiveness for that sin. "God, I ask You to forgive me for the sin of [*name it*] in my life."

3. Read the Scripture that promises forgiveness to those who confess (1 John 1:9).

4. Ask them, "Do you know that God forgives you?" Wait for a response.

5. Announce, with eye contact: "In the name of Jesus Christ, you are forgiven."

Close the session with prayer.

Teaching Chapter VIII
"FORGIVENESS AND THE HEALING PROCESS"

Open the session with prayer.

Read aloud the session's introductory statement.

Read the Scripture story in Matthew 18:23–35.

Work through the materials on what forgiveness is and what it is not, so that class members may have an adequate understanding of its nature.

Forgiveness is grounded in the nature of God as demonstrated in the life of Jesus Christ. It is important to help persons understand that forgiveness is an act of God's will and is initiated by God.

Discuss how forgiveness functioned in and through the life of Jesus. This lays the foundation for how forgiveness works in the lives of individual persons.

Utilize the reflection section at the conclusion of the chapter.

Close the session with prayer.

Teaching Chapter IX
"PRACTICING FORGIVENESS"

Read aloud the chapter's introductory statements.

It is suggested that the first half of this session be used to discuss the material in the class manual: forgiveness between an individual and God, forgiveness between persons, and forgiveness of self.

The second half of the class session is a workshop in which persons get into groups of three. Follow the same process as suggested for chapter IV: one sharing and two listening.

As the facilitator, read aloud the questions at the conclusion of the chapter after the groups are formed.

Each person in the small group will have opportunity to say:

"[*Name*], I forgive you for [*name the offense*]."

"God, I ask You to forgive me for my attitude [*name the attitude*] toward [*name*]."

Others in the small group will ask, "Do you know you are forgiven?" "Will you accept God's forgiveness?" "In the name of Jesus Christ, you are forgiven."

Close the workshop session with prayer.

Teaching Chapter X
"HEALING OF EMOTIONAL HURTS"

Open the session with prayer.

Read aloud the session's introductory statements.

Read the Scriptures, prepared to utilize the material included in the manual. It is critical that the information be imparted to the members of the class. Class members may follow in their manual as the material is being covered.

We suggest that facilitator and class members alike add their own personal stories throughout the material.

IMPORTANT NOTATION FOR FACILITATOR: The one additional step that is included in this session, beyond the forgiveness of the ones who offend, is that of asking the Holy Spirit to give a vision of Jesus in the scene of the offense. Emphasize that this is *not* conjuring up pictures or visualizing an imaginary thing. This is an honest seeking to see Jesus present in the situation.

Allow plenty of time for discussion of the reflection section. This discussion will prepare the class for the workshop on emotional healing.

Follow the workshop process that is outlined on pages 73–75, with emphasis on step 4.

Teaching Chapter XI
"THE GIFT OF DISCERNMENT"

Open the session with prayer.

Read aloud the session's introductory statement.

Read the related Scripture passage(s).

Read and discuss the various levels of discernment. Help the class members differentiate between natural and spiritual discernment and also the spiritual gift of discernment.

The facilitator will want to become familiar with the Bible stories and other Scriptures that emphasize the gift of discernment. Short (twenty-five words or less) personal stories from class members are also appropriate.

Use the questions at the end of the chapter as a guide for discussion.

Close the session with prayer.

Teaching Chapter XII
"THE MINISTRY OF DELIVERANCE"

Open the session with prayer.

Read the related Scripture passage(s).

Following the material in the book will provide information and an opportunity for discussion among the members of the class.

Since some may not be familiar with the demonic or deliverance, it will be important to allow plenty of time for class members to express their understanding and how they feel about the subject.

Try to help them understand that 100 percent of Jesus' ministry involved deliverance of some kind.

- He brought people out of the kingdom of darkness into the kingdom of light.
- He delivered them:
  - from ignorance to understanding.
  - from the letter of the law to the spirit of the law.
  - from hatred to love.
  - from bondage to freedom.

About one-fourth of Jesus' ministry was involved in delivering people from bondage to the demonic. He was truly the Deliverer and His was a deliverance ministry.

It will be helpful for participants to also recall the Scripture in Ephesians 6:12 that states that our struggle is not against people but against principalities and powers in the heavenly realms.

Use the reflection section at the end of the chapter to give direction for the discussion.

Close the session with prayer.

Teaching Chapter XIII
"PHYSICAL HEALING"

Open the session with prayer.

Read aloud the session's introductory statement.

Read the related Scripture passage(s).

It may be helpful to have handouts prepared in advance, listing the five kinds of healing and the three levels of healing.

This and earlier chapters are designed to disseminate information in preparation for the discussion and prayer for physical healing. That will be a workshop in which class members will have opportunity to pray for one another for physical healing.

When the study material has been covered, use the reflection section at the end of the chapter.

Close the session with prayer.

Teaching Chapter XIV
"THE PHYSICAL HEALING PROCESS"

Open the session with prayer.

Read aloud the session's introductory statement.

Read the related Scripture passage(s).

The facilitator is crucial in helping class members understand the healing process and the ways in which healing occurs. Go through the material step by step, discussing questions that may be asked.

Usually persons have questions related to the fact that not all persons are healed. Save plenty of time for discussion of death and healing. Emphasize the fact that death is *not* a healing, but our healing is in the resurrection. Help the class members understand the New Testament Scriptures related to death (listed in the book).

Follow the reflection questions at the end of the chapter.

Begin the workshop with prayer for the entire group.

Sample prayer: "O God, You know the thoughts of our hearts, our desire for healing and wholeness, and our plan to pray for one another. We thank You that Your desire is that we be whole in spirit, mind, and body. We know You as our Healer and we know that we pray within Your will as we pray for healing. Thank You for Your presence that brings life. Help us to be sensitive to Your voice and to the needs of those who seek healing. Anoint us with Your healing Spirit in order that Your perfect will may be done. Through Jesus Christ our Lord. Amen."

Instruct the students to gather into groups of two or three, and to share their needs for physical healing with their group or prayer partner

Follow the instructions listed in the workshop on page 104.

Let the participants share healings that happened as a result of the prayer time.

Note: As this is the last session/chapter of the book, you should set aside a ten- to twenty-minute (or longer) portion at the end of the meeting to recap, answer questions, and discuss the overall study and various workshop sessions.

As the facilitator, you should plan a follow-up session with the participants six to eight weeks following the last workshop. This will provide participants an opportunity to report on the fruit they've experienced since completing the study and also allow you to answer any new questions that may have arisen.

Close the session with prayer.

BIBLIOGRAPHY

Deliverance:

MacNutt, Francis. *Deliverance from Evil Spirits—A Practical Manual.* Grand Rapids, Mich.: Chosen Books Publishing Co., 1995.

McAll, Kenneth. *Healing the Family Tree.* London: Sheldon Press, 1986.

Sandford, John and Mark Sandford. *Comprehensive Guide to Deliverances and Inner Healing.* Grand Rapids, Mich.: Chosen Books Publishing Co., 1992.

White, Thomas B. *The Believer's Guide to Spiritual Warfare.* Ann Arbor, Mich.: Servant Publications, 1990.

Forgiveness:

Augsburger, David. *The Freedom of Forgiveness.* Chicago, Ill.: Moody Press, 1970.

Cook, Jerry with Stanley C. Baldwin. *Love, Acceptance and Forgiveness.* Ventura, Calif.: Regal Books/Gospel Light Publications, 1980.

Donnelly, Doris. *Learning to Forgive.* Nashville, Tenn.: Abingdon Press, 1982.

———. *Putting Forgiveness into Practice.* Allen, Tex.: Argus Communications, 1982.

Lilly, Gene. *God is Calling His People to Forgiveness.* Houston, Tex.: Hunter Ministries Publishers, 1977.

Morrisey, Kirkie. *A Woman's Workshop on Forgiveness.* Grand Rapids, Mich.: Zondervan Publishers, 1982.

Nieder, John and Thomas M. Thompson. *Forgive and Love Again.* Eugene, Ore.: Harvest House Publisher, 1991.

Ogilvie, Lloyd John. *You are Loved and Forgiven.* Ventura, Calif.: Regal Books/Gospel Light Publications, 1977.

Healing:

Dossey, Larry. *Healing Words.* New York, N.Y.: Harper Collins Publishers, 1993.

Hunter, Charles and Frances Hunter. *How to Heal the Sick.* Kingswood, Tex.: Hunter Books, 1981.

MacNutt, Francis. *The Prayer that Heals.* Notre Dame, Ind.: Ave Maria Press, 1981.

Ogilvie, Lloyd John. *You Can Pray with Power.* Ventura, Calif.: Regal Books/Gospel Light Publications, 1988.

Payne, Leanne. *The Healing Presence.* Westchester, Ill.: Crossway Books, 1989.

Pearson, Mark A. *Christian Healing.* Grand Rapids, Mich.: Chosen Books/Baker Book House, 1995.

"Signs and Wonders Today," *Christian Life Magazine.* Wheaton, Ill.: Christian Life Mission, 1983.

Wagner, C. Peter. *How to Have a Healing Ministry Without Making Your Church Sick*. Ventura, Calif.: Regal Books/Gospel Light Publications, 1988.

Holy Spirit:

Barclay, William. *The Promise of the Spirit*. Philadelphia, Penn.: The Westminster Press, 1976.
Basham, Don. *A Handbook on Holy Spirit Baptism*. Monroeville, Penn.: Whitaker Books, 1969.
———. *Ministering the Baptism in the Holy Spirit*. Monroeville, Penn.: Whitaker Books, 1971.
Beall, James Lee. *The School of the Holy Spirit*. Monroeville, Penn.: Whitaker Books, 1971.
Bennett, Dennis. *The Holy Spirit and You*. Plainfield, N.J.: Logos International, 1971.
———. *Moving Right Along with the Holy Spirit*. Old Tappan, N.J.: Fleming H. Revell Company, 1983.
———. *Nine O'Clock in the Morning*. Plainfield, N.J.: Logos International, 1970.
Cho, Paul Yonggi. *The Holy Spirit, My Senior Partner*. Altamonte, Fla.: Creation House, 1989.
Christiansen, Larry. *Speaking in Tongues*. Minneapolis, Minn.: Dimension Books/Bethany Fellowship, 1968.
Custer, Chester E. and Mack B. Stokes. *The Holy Spirit in the Wesleyan Heritage, Teacher and Student Guide*. Nashville, Tenn.: Graded Press, 1985.
Deere, Jack. *Surprised by the Spirit*. Grand Rapids, Mich.: Zondervan Publishing, 1993.
DuPlessis, David. *The Spirit Bade Me Go*. Oakland, Calif.: David DuPlessis, 1963.
Hinn, Benny. *Good Morning, Holy Spirit*. Nashville, Tenn.: Thomas Nelson, Inc., 1990.
Sanders, Oswald. *The Pursuit of the Holy Spirit*. Grand Rapids, Mich.: Zondervan Publishing House, 1972.
Shoemaker, Samuel A. *With the Holy Spirit and With Fire*. New York, N.Y.: Harper Brothers, 1960.
Stokes, Mack B. *The Holy Spirit in the Wesleyan Heritage*. Nashville, Tenn.: Graded Press, 1985.
Torrey, R. A. *The Person and Work of the Holy Spirit*. New Kensington, Penn.: Whitaker House, 1996.

Inner Healing:

Arthur, Kay. *Lord, Heal My Hurts*. Portland, Ore.: Multnomah Press, 1988.
Bennett, Rita. *How to Pray for Inner Healing for Yourself and Others*. Old Tappan, N.J.: Fleming H. Revell Co. 1983.
———. *Inner Wholeness Through the Lord's Prayer*. Tarrytown, N.Y.: Chosen Books/Fleming H. Revell Co., 1991.
———. *Making Peace with Your Inner Child*. Old Tappan, NJ: Power Books/Fleming H. Revell Co., 1987.
———. *You Can Be Emotionally Free*. Old Tappan, N.J.: Power Books/Fleming H. Revell Co., 1982.
Colbert, Don. *Deadly Emotions*. Nashville, Tenn.: Thomas Nelson, Inc., 2003.
Davis, Ron Lee. *Healing Life's Hurts*. Dallas, Tex.: Word Publishing, 1986.
Dearing, Trevor. *God and Healing of the Mind*. South Plainfield, N.J.: Bridge Publishing Co., 1983.
Flynn, Mike and Doug Gregg. *Inner Healing*. Downer Grove, Ill.: InterVarsity Press, 1993.
Hormann, Aiko. *Overcomers' Reference Book*. Santa Monica, Calif.: Aiko Hormann Ministries, 2001.
Linn, Dennis and Michael Linn. *Healing Life's Hurts*. New York, N.Y.: Paulist Press, 1978.
———. *Healing of Memories*. New York, N.Y.: Paulist Press, 1974.

Linn, Matthew, Dennis Linn, and Sheila Fabricant. *Healing the Greatest Hurt.* Makwah, N.Y.: Paulist Press, 1985.

Parkhurst, Genevieve. *Five Loaves and Two Fishes—New Life Through Inner Healing.* Plainfield, N.J: Logos International, 1978.

———. *Positive Living Through Inner Healing.* Plainfield, N.J.: Logos International, 1978.

Price, Charles S. *Experiencing the Father's Embrace.* Lake Mary, Fla.: Mercy Place, 1952.

———. *The Meaning of Faith.* Shippenburg, Penn.: Mercy Place, 2002.

Sandford, John and Paula Sandford. *The Elijah Task.* Plainfield, N.J.: Logos, 1977.

———. *Healing the Wounded Spirit.* South Plainfield, N.J.: Bridge Publishing Co., 1985.

———. *The Transformation of the Inner Man.* South Plainfield, N.J.: Bridge Publishing Co., 1982.

Sandford, Paula. *Healing Women's Emotions.* Tulsa, Okla.: Victory House, 1992.

Sanford, Agnes. *The Healing Light.* Shakopea, Minn.: Macalster Park Publishing Co., 1922.

Savard, Liberty. *The Unsurrendered Soul.* Gainesville, Fla.: Bridge Logos, 2002.

Seamands, David A. *Healing for Damaged Emotions.* Wheaton, Ill.: Victor Books, 1986.

———. *Healing of Memories.* Wheaton, Ill.: Victor Books, SP Publications, Inc., 1985.

———. *Putting Away Childish Things.* Wheaton, Ill.: Victor Books, 1985.

Shlemon, Barbara Leaky. *Healing the Hidden Self.* Notre Dame, Ind.: Ave Maria Press, 1982.

Tapscott, Betty. *Ministering Inner Healing.* Houston, Tex.: Tapscott Ministries, 1987.

Wright, Henry W. *A More Excellent Way.* Thomaston, Ga.: Pleasant Valley Publications, 2003.

General:

Seamands, David A. *God's Blueprint for Living.* Wilmore, Ky.: Bristol Books, 1989.

ABOUT THE AUTHORS

Married shortly after graduating high school, Larry and Audrey Eddings have been involved in ministry for more than half a century. Larry was ordained an Elder in the Methodist Church and has pastored numerous churches in several states. In 1983, he was appointed General Evangelist in The United Methodist Church. Audrey was ordained by Grace Church, an independent denomination, and ministers in the area of healing emotional hurts.

Larry earned a bachelor of science degree from Lewis and Clark College in Portland, Oregon, and later a bachelor of divinity degree from Garret Biblical Institute in Evanston, Illinois. Audrey Eddings studied at Denver University in Denver, Colorado; Valley College in San Bernadino, California; Olympic College in Bremerton, Washington; and Oral Roberts University in Tulsa, Oklahoma.

In 1971, Larry and Audrey were baptized with the Holy Spirit. Since that experience, they have been active in the Holy Spirit renewal ministry. Both have served on the board—Larry served as president and Audrey as vice-president—and council of Aldersgate Renewal Ministries, an affiliate of the General Board of Discipleship of The United Methodist Church. They are members of the National Association of United Methodist Evangelists, of which Larry also served as president.

The couple founded Wind of the Spirit Ministries in 1983, and have conducted healing academies, wholeness seminars and workshops, conferences on the Holy Spirit, prayer retreats, local church training and ministry events, and international missions. They have ministered throughout the United States and in Canada, Nigeria, the Philippines, Paraguay, and Mexico. Materials they have written are used as curriculum at the Paraguay Bible Institute and at other institutions.

Residents of Silverdale, Washington, Larry and Audrey continue to tell others of the healing power of the Holy Spirit. They have two children and seven grandchildren.